# LOVED

The One Truth That Every Person Needs To Hear

## JOHN ANDREWS

RIVER
PUBLISHING

River Publishing & Media Ltd
info@river-publishing.co.uk

ISBN 978-1-908393-82-1

# Contents

# Dedication

Beth-Anne Ruth

*Last but never least.*

As my third jewel you have completed my crown.
May you always live in the knowledge of His love, experiencing
the freedom of His love and touching a dying world with the
power of His love.

**I love you.**

*"But from everlasting to everlasting the Lord's love is with those who
fear Him, and His righteousness with their children's children – with
those who keep His covenant and remember to obey His precepts."*
(Psalm 103:17-18)

# Acknowledgements

Writing *Loved* has proved to be a deeply moving experience. Often, as words hit the screen, I found myself pausing to worship and express my gratitude to God, as well as wipe tears from my eyes on more than one occasion.

However, nothing of consequence happens without the support and contribution of outstanding friends. Here are just a few of them.

To Dawn: you are amazing. The more I live with you the more grateful I am to God that He found you for me. Your love, encouragement and sacrifice continually inspire me and because of you I am rich beyond words. I love you.

To my children, Elaina, Simeon and Beth-Anne: may you always know you are loved without condition!

To everyone who contributed to my journey in understanding the love of God, I thank you.

To my heavenly Father, who loved me before the foundations of the earth were even laid. Thank you for loving me and helping me to begin the process of understanding just how much you love me. I look forward to discovering more about your awesome love.

# Preface

Lorna would stand at her window and look enviously at the people passing by. Often she'd remark to her husband, Ken, "I wish I had a life." She had spent most of her life giving to others, but with her children grown up and the best part of sixty-seven years on planet earth behind her, she was empty. Her journey for a life brought her to our church, where she attended for a number of months, coming and going without any change.

One Sunday morning she sat and listened politely and intently to the sermon. The preacher that day was speaking on the power of love. In particular, the fact that God's love comes without any strings attached.

"He loves you without condition, without reservation and without limitation," he proclaimed. "He loves you, full stop!"

In a moment, Lorna's life was transformed by this simple yet profound revelation. For the first time in her life she understood an immense truth: "God loves me!" On the way home in the car Lorna kept saying over and over to Ken, "Jesus loves me, Jesus loves me, Jesus loves me!!!"

One of the first verses of the Bible I ever memorized was John 3:16. It says,

*"For God so loved the world that He gave His one and only Son, that whoever believes in Him shall not perish but have eternal life."*

However, I have discovered an amazing truth: Jesus didn't just die for the world, He died for me and He loves me passionately and unreservedly. The knowledge of His love has granted me freedom, wholeness, joy and a quality of life which is beyond my wildest dreams. His love has taken me to places I never thought I'd go and taught me lessons I never thought possible to learn. I am blessed with every spiritual blessing in Christ Jesus and I have been enriched in every way, due to no other reason than the fact that God has lavished His love on me.

This book is a meager attempt to celebrate the one truth above all that humanity needs to hear: *that we are loved by God.* In the following chapters I hope to unearth for you a jewel of priceless wonder, which once possessed will banish everything of transient value into its shadow. The message of this book is simple: *you are loved!* My hope is that you will truly discover His love, just like Lorna, and experience through His love the life for which you were created. As you read, open your heart and dare to believe that the rumours are true. God is love and He loves you!

*"And I ask Him that with both feet planted firmly on love, you'll be able to take in with all followers of Jesus the extravagant dimensions of Christ's love. Reach out and experience the breadth! Test its length! Plumb the depths! Rise to the heights! Live full lives, full in the fullness of God."*
(Ephesians 3:17-19 MSG)

*Dr John Andrews*

# Chapter 1
## World-Changing Words

"By love alone is God enjoyed by love alone delighted in,
by love alone approached and admired."[1]

My children have a book called *Find Freddie*. It is filled with page after page of detailed pictures in all manner of settings and the aim is to find the little man called *Freddie*. He's somewhere in there wearing his red jumper with a large orange F on the front, sporting a bright green scarf around his lovely little neck. Each page reveals a new setting into which Freddie blends – everything from outer space to school to the beach; not to mention my personal favourite, the museum. I thought to myself, "How hard can it be to find such a character?" After all, the F on Freddie's jumper is so bright it has been known to confuse approaching airplanes. I played this game *once* with my children and approached it with a fair degree of confidence. The truth is that by the end of my "quality fun-time" with the kids, I had gone cross-eyed, my head hurt, I'd accused them of lying to me (convinced that Freddie was not on the page) and got to the place where if I ever found Freddie he would be sorry!

---

1. Thomas Traherne.

The source of my frustration was that I knew Freddie was there, but I just could not find him. He wasn't hiding from me, he was right in front of my eyes, but what a struggle it was to see and find him.

The last three words of 1 John 4:8 form one of the most profound and amazing statements in the whole Bible, as well as being one of the hardest to believe. John proclaims confidently: *"God is love!"* John, like the other writers of the Bible, invites us to open up the Book and find God, the God of love. Yet my experience is that both within and without the Church, many struggle to find *the God that is Love.* Over the years I have met and ministered to many people who attend church, read the Bible and know the creed, but can't seem to spot the God who is love. Talk about judgement, justice, discipline, sin, sickness and suffering, and their eyes come clearly into focus and Bible verses pop out of their mouths. On such topics they are comfortable. However, when it comes to the God who is love, they know He is on the page somewhere... but they just can't see Him.

Before we go any further, consider these questions:

*When you are looking for God, who are you looking for and what do you see?*

*Do you expect to be surprised by His love and mercy, or are you waiting for the frown, the rebuke or the rod?*

Take a moment to read 1 John 4:7-21.

### An appalling truth?

Twice in the passage we are told "God is love" (4:8 & 16). John is not merely identifying one of God's qualities, he is making an absolute statement about the essence of *who God is.* Already he has told us that God is light (1:5) and God is righteous (2:29), but in this statement, "God is love", everything else is eclipsed. This is the most breathtaking, awe-inspiring expression of God's very nature. To grasp this is to find God and discover life.

*The Screwtape Letters*, by C.S. Lewis, contains the imagined correspondence between a senior devil called Screwtape to a junior devil, his nephew, Wormwood. In it the younger is instructed by the older in the art of distracting those who seek to follow Jesus, by using whatever means necessary to win the battle for each soul. Throughout the letters references are made to the love of God. Screwtape is convinced that all "His (God's) talk about Love must be a disguise for something else – He must have some *real* motive for creating them and taking so much trouble about them."[2] Unaccustomed to the concept of love, Screwtape cannot get his head around the idea of God showing any love towards humanity. "We know that He cannot really love; nobody can; it doesn't make sense."[3] Though he does not understand it, Screwtape reluctantly accepts it and warns his young nephew, "One must face the fact that all the talk about His love for men, and His service being perfect freedom, is not (as one would gladly believe) mere propaganda, but *an appalling truth*."[4]

I love that last expression "an appalling truth". For Screwtape, whose mind is set on the destruction of humanity, the thought that someone could love so recklessly, without the slightest hint of a hidden agenda at work, is beyond his comprehension. Sadly, he is not alone. Ironically, even within the Church it is this *appalling truth* which stumbles so many.

To be loved without condition is, for some, too much for their mind – an equation that simply does not compute. Tragically,

---

2. Lewis, C.S., *The Screwtape Letters*, 1942, p.97, (My insertion in brackets).
3. Ibid., p.98.
4. Ibid., p.45. My italics.

outside the Church this *appalling truth* is rarely heard by millions who need to hear it, perhaps concluding that if there is a God, He is angry, irrelevant and uninterested in them. The truth that God is love has become for them an appalling joke!

When I was in Bible College, I had the privilege of studying theology and I confess I enjoyed the numerous arguments which followed. One area of study was on the nature and character of God. I ploughed my way through Louis Berkhof's *Systematic Theology* (finding Freddie was easier), making copious notes and coming to the confident conclusion that I knew all about God. I got to know about the *essential attributes* of God. As the name suggests, these are the qualities which essentially belong to Him. Six essential qualities of God were drilled into me: God is eternal, He is self-existent, He is unchanging (immutable), He is all-powerful (omnipotent), all-knowing (omniscient) and He is everywhere at once (omnipresent). Then I learned about His *moral attributes*: the qualities which belong to Him relating especially to His creation. These included His holiness, righteousness, love, goodness, grace, mercy, compassion and kindness.

As important as all these qualities are, and as valuable as it is to study and examine them individually, I have come to the conclusion that they all hinge on love. Love is not just one of God's attributes, it is essentially who God is. Love is at the heart of God's nature. God not only has love, He *is* love. Try to imagine the six essential qualities of God without love? Would humanity have even gotten out of the Garden of Eden if the all-powerful, all-knowing God had not been in very nature, love? Try to imagine God's moral balance if it was not governed by love. We can have confidence in God's power because God is love. His love governs His power, thus protecting creation and humanity from fitful moments of impatience and frustration. Imagine the consequences if God, who is unchanging, did not have love at the centre of His being? His love forms the foundation and framework on which His essential attributes hang. The eternal, all-knowing, all-powerful, all-present, unchanging God, is not only a God who loves, but He *is* love. As a result, we can have confidence in His judgements and His actions. They are not random acts. Rather they are governed and administered out of an unshakable code of love. God is good because He is love. God is gracious because He is love. God shows mercy because He is love. All that He is, is held together in love and all that He does is an expression of love.

The movie *Bruce Almighty* is the story of a man who gets the chance to be God for a period of time. Predictably, it is the prospect of unlimited power which initially gives the newly crowned master of the universe his greatest buzz. But Bruce soon discovers that power is not enough to run the world. Prayer requests start to bombard him via email. At first he tries to read each one, but so many are hitting his system that he makes a unilateral decision: he says yes to everyone! It sounds simple; everyone will be happy and Bruce can get on with whatever God-types do when they are not attending to humanity.

If the only thing God had going for Him was power we would be in big trouble. The Bible declares that He created the universe and that He sustains it by the *"word of His power."* However, it is not only His power that is keeping the universe spinning, it is His love. Bruce had the power to say yes to every request – and so does God. The difference between Bruce and God is this: God not only reads every email sent to Him, but He passionately loves every sender. Bruce wanted to get on with other things, but for God, you are His main thing. Bruce soon realised that being God wasn't that easy because for most of the movie he was thinking about himself, whereas God spends His time *thinking about us!*

**Shush, it's a secret**

For years my brother Alex and I kept a dark secret. During one of those long summers when kids are off school and generally have nothing to do, tensions began to rise between my beloved big brother and me. Being five years older, he did not always want me hanging around and, to be fair, I was a bit of a pain. One particular dispute got a little out of control and I ended up being locked out of the house. As I screamed to be let in, my anger reached boiling point and I took it out on the front door. As my fist crashed against the window panel it shattered and at that moment everything stopped. Suddenly, as my life flashed before my eyes and I considered the impending judgement from my "pain first, ask questions later" mother, anger was replaced by fear and I needed a toilet... quickly!

A conspiracy was hatched and although my brother and I had been sworn enemies a few minutes previously, we were now united by a common fear of death. We concocted a story that we believed would save both our lives. The story involved a passing car, a piece of loose stone on the road, and a one in a million probability that the car could flip the stone up and smash the window. The fact that I am writing the story for you means my mother bought it (or so we thought).

A number of years later I was leaving to go to Bible College and decided to confess this deed of darkness. I could not go off to my holy calling with such a crime on my pure soul. As I started to tell the story, my mother began to laugh. She had known all along. She had spoken to a neighbour who had told her everything. So why hadn't she executed vengeance upon us? She was so impressed by our loyalty and love for each other in sticking to the story, and in keeping it a secret, that she decided to do nothing.

The dictionary defines a secret as something, "kept or to be kept from general knowledge or view, hidden from all or all but a few, unrevealed, covert, confidential."[5]

Why is the God who is love, one of the best-kept secrets in the universe? One would think that such a truth would be celebrated and enjoyed in the Church and trumpeted and proclaimed to a dying world. Yet somehow, this glorious truth, this life-giving message, this world-changing power, has been among the most neglected in pulpits and in mission.

Victor Hugo, the French poet, novelist and dramatist, was born in 1802. His parents had set their hearts on a baby girl, even picking a name for her: *Victorine*. When *he* was born, in disappointment they shortened the name to *Victor*. The two works with which people will most readily associate him are *Les Miserables* and *The Hunchback of Notre-Dame*. Both of these immensely powerful works express and proclaim the virtues of truth, justice, mercy, grace and, above all, love. In both books there are some pivotal moments.

In *Les Miserables*, Jean Valjean served a nineteen-year prison term. Having earned his release, he was confronted by a world that did not care much for criminals. A bishop took him in and Valjean promptly repaid his love by robbing him. The thief was quickly captured and brought before the bishop, facing the prospect of a lifetime in prison. It is at this moment that something truly incredible happened.

The bishop offered Valjean his candlesticks to add to the silver he had already stolen and not only forgave him, but through an act of unrestrained love, offered him hope and an opportunity to change.

---

5. *Pocket Oxford Dictionary*, 1969.

This second chance became the first day of the rest of Valjean's life as one transformed by the love of God demonstrated through the bishop.

In *The Hunchback of Notre-Dame*, Quasimodo is described as a "monster of deformity". Ugly and unusual, he lived a lonely and isolated life within the confines of his home – the Cathedral at Notre-Dame. Ironically, a place intended for sanctuary, acceptance and healing, it had become his prison house, but one which he longed to venture from. In one particularly horrible scene Quasimodo was caught by the crowd, having to endure their taunts and jeers for over an hour; his cry for water was ignored by the heartless crowd. This was humanity at its worst. Just then a beautiful young woman, Esmeralda, approached him, courageously defying the crowd and producing a flask of water. She applied it, "…to the lips of the exhausted wretch." In the midst of barbarity, Quasimodo experienced the touch of love at the hands of this girl and the baying hordes were stunned by an act of love that both inspired and shamed.

Hugo lived in a cruel and indifferent world where the weak were trampled, the deformed were despised, and second chances were rarely dispensed. Yet through his parables he sought to reveal the well-kept secret that God is love, as demonstrated through the candlesticks of the bishop and the water of a dancing girl.

When God wanted to reveal the secret of His love He sent His Son. Jesus' mission was not only to save the world by dying for it, but also to demonstrate to the world the immensity of the love of God. He came not to condemn but to give life. He came not for the healthy and the righteous, but for the sick and sinners. He spent time with people that well-respected religious-types would never associate with and touched people deemed untouchable.

So if the message is out… why is it still such a secret?

**Lost in translation**

Whilst travelling I discovered the following mis-translated signs in an airplane magazine:

*Paris hotel elevator*: Please leave your values at the front desk. If you lose them in your room, we are not responsible.

*Athens hotel*: Visitors are expected to complain at the office between the hours of 9 and 11 a.m. daily.

*Yugoslavian hotel*: The flattening of underwear with pleasure is the job of the chambermaid.

*Moscow hotel*: You are welcome to visit the cemetery where famous Russian and Soviet composers, artists and writers are buried daily except Thursday.

*Bangkok dry cleaners*: Drop your trousers here for best results.

*Greek tailor shop*: Order your summer suit. Because of the big rush we will execute customers in strict rotation.

*Copenhagen airline*: We take your bags and send them in all directions.

*Moscow hotel*: If this is your first visit to Russia, you are welcome to it.

*Norwegian lounge*: Ladies are requested not to have children in the bar.

And finally, my personal favourite;

*Tokyo car rental firm*: When passenger with heavy foot is in sight, tootle the horn. Trumpet him melodiously at first, but if he still obstacles your passage, then tootle him with vigour.

Going back to *Find Freddie*, my children are good at it. They find him in double-quick time, because they know where he is. I thought it was down to their astute powers of observation when it was much more simple than that. Having previously found him, they knew where he was and they couldn't understand why I was taking so long to see something that was obvious to them. Having read the Bible and found the God who is love, I now see Him on every page. Now I just can't understand why others don't see him. "He's there, right in front of you."

How is it that a message so pregnant with love from the dawn of time has somehow been lost in translation, so that the God represented in the Bible looks and sounds nothing like the God of love? What have we been seeing? What have we been preaching and teaching? What message have we been giving to those outside the Church?

In Bible College revival was a subject not far from all our lips. We read about it, prayed about it and were convinced that we, like no generation before us, would usher it in! One of the men celebrated in this context was Jonathan Edwards. He was an American theologian, minister and missionary and was influential in the Great Awakening of the 1740s. He did many things and preached thousands of sermons, but it was one sermon in particular which evoked great imagination. It's title was *Sinners in the Hands of an Angry God* from the text Deuteronomy 32:35. I have read that sermon and, although I do not wish to judge something out of the context of its time, a number of things are striking. Firstly, humanity is seen as wicked, undeserving of anything but hell and judgement. Secondly, God is seen as eager and ready to exact judgement whenever possible. For instance,

"He is not only able to cast wicked men into hell, but he can most easily do it."[6]

Later Edwards added, "God has laid himself under no obligation, by a promise, to keep any natural man out of hell one moment."[7]

---

6. *Jonathan Edwards on Knowing Christ*, 1990 (sermon volume from 1839), p.184.
7. Edwards, op.cit., p.188.

The sermon is saturated with imagery of vengeance, justice and punishment. There is only one small reference to God's love and even that is in the context of judgement. With unerring clarity, Edwards builds to a horrific conclusion:

> "The God that holds you over the pit of hell, much as one holds a spider, or some loathsome insect, over the fire, abhors you, and is dreadfully provoked: his wrath towards you burns like fire; he looks upon you as worthy of nothing else, but to be cast into the fire..."[8]

Why do I highlight this? For years this type of sermon was the benchmark of my upbringing. The harder and heavier we preached about hell and damnation the better, convinced that this was the way to get people's attention. For years we stood in open-air missions and screamed insults at people doing their shopping, wondering why they wouldn't take our tracts, shake our hands or come to our churches. Could it be something got lost in translation?!

It seems to me that Jesus never once used fear, hell or judgement to motivate people to follow Him. Instead, He set forth His claims and then asked them to follow Him. Incredibly, many did. One day He approached a young tax-collector called Matthew. He asked Matthew to follow Him and the Bible says that Matthew left everything and did so. That night, to celebrate his new found faith and freedom, Matthew threw a party for all his sinner friends and Jesus was chief guest. Words like hell, judgement, wretch, abhor and worthless were never used. Many experienced the touch of heaven in a way they had never expected. They received a new translation of an old truth.

---

8. Ibid., p.191.

I looked again at some of the creeds of the early Church, namely The Apostles' Creed (end of second century), The Nicene Creed (from the fourth century) and The Gallican Creed (from the sixth century). In the midst of the magnificent theology there is not a single reference to the love of God. The denomination of which I am a part has a list of fundamental beliefs and, again, there is no clear reference to the God of love. My point is not a criticism of the great creeds or my denominational beliefs, but rather an observation that as the Church we assume we are talking about the love of God and that the world knows we know about the love of God. But when we look a bit closer at what we claim to believe and listen carefully to what we're actually preaching, the message is not as clear as we think.

The preacher sat jet-lagged in a quiet little diner in down-town Hawaii. Having just flown in and unable to sleep, a cup of coffee and a piece of pie seemed inviting. As he ate, two young women, dressed to kill, entered the diner. They ordered coffee and sat either side of the preacher and talked about their night's work. Their talk was loud and crude and, feeling uncomfortable, the preacher decided to move. As he was about to do so he overheard that one of them, Agnes, would be 39 the next day. Her friend responded in a nasty tone, "So what do you want from me, a birthday party?" "Come on," said Agnes, "why do you have to be so mean? I was just telling you, that's all. Why do you have to put me down? I was just telling you it was my birthday. I don't want anything from you. I mean, why should you give me a birthday party? I've never had a birthday party in my whole life. Why should I have one now?"

When the girls left, the preacher approached the guy behind the counter and inquired after them. Yes, he knew them, they were regulars, prostitutes. The preacher suggested that they throw a birthday party for the young woman. The plan was laid and the party prepared.

The next night the girls came in bang on time and with great surprise the trap was sprung. Agnes experienced her first birthday party. She was given a huge cake and was stunned by "love" of a different kind. She had never been treated with respect by a man before. The only time men had been nice to her was to get something.

As the party continued, the waiter discovered that the man was a preacher. "Hey! You never told me you were a preacher. What kind of church do you belong to?"

"I belong to a church that throws birthday parties for whores at 3.30am in the morning," the preacher replied.

"No you don't," the waiter responded. "There's no such church like that. If there was, I'd join it. *I'd join a church like that!*"[9]

God is love! The phrase seems so small and easy to miss in the millions of words printed in the Bible. Three words on a page can so easily merge into the rest and, if we are not careful, we can find ourselves reading the Bible without ever really seeing them. It's time to open up the Bible and, with it, your heart. Play a game with me. We're going to spend time looking for the God who is love. He's in there, somewhere and if we are diligent we'll find Him. Once we find Him, we'll see Him on every page of the Book and I guarantee, once experienced, His love will transform our outlook and lifestyle forever. These three words have the power to change our world and God knows it needs it.

---

9. Campolo, T., *The Kingdom of God is a Party*, Word, 1990, pp. 4-9. My italics.

# Chapter 2
# Extravagant Dimensions

"Dear God, I bet it is very hard for you to love all of everybody in the whole world. There are only four people in our family and I can never do it."[1]

William was thirty-two years old and his brother Ian was thirty-five, but they would always need their parents. Though Ian was older and in good physical health, he was trapped in the mind of a four-year-old, while his younger brother, William, who was able to do more for himself than Ian, had the mind of a fourteen to fifteen-year-old boy. I've never met these young men, but I met their mum, Tina, who at that time had been married to Sandy for thirty-six years and was one of those modest, unassuming, remarkable heroes who manages to "turn up" every day and do whatever has to be done to make life, marriage, family and friendship work. By day she worked as a credit controller in the accounts department of a garage, and the rest of the time she's a devoted wife to Sandy and a mother to the two sons she adores.

Over the years they have faced many struggles and heartaches, contending with the reactions of others, fuelled by ignorance, as well as the pain caused by opinions saturated in sarcasm. In

---

1. *Children's Letters to God*, 1991. These words are from Nan.

spite of this, Tina and Sandy have managed to keep going and keep loving. I asked her if she had ever considered giving up and walking away from her "life of routine". Her answer was emphatic. "No! There's no way. They are my sons and that's it!" I was interested to know what motivated her to keep going. In a world where broken things get discarded and where the cult of self rejects the inconvenience of suffering, I wanted to discover how this *ordinary* woman had managed to survive and succeed in the light of the challenges she faced. Her conclusion was profound yet simple: "Love," she said, "just keeps on growing… we all know that!"[2]

I have been on the planet long enough to understand that love in the dimensions Tina describes is a rare commodity. Rich and poor, oppressed and free, white and black, whatever our label, all of us deep down long for the touch of love and for the health and healing it brings. In the eyes of society, William and Ian would be classed as the unlucky victims of a genetic collision, but I say they are among the most blessed people on earth, because they are loved and they know it.

In one of his letters, Paul wrote these words:

*"And I pray that you, being rooted and established in love, may have the power, together with all the saints, to grasp how wide and long and high and deep is the love of Christ, and to know this love that surpasses knowledge – that you may be filled to the measure of all the fulness of God."* (Ephesians 3:17-19)

I love how the Message puts these verses:

*"And I ask Him that with both feet planted firmly on love, you'll be able to take in with all Christians the extravagant dimensions of Christ's love. Reach out and experience the breadth! Test its*

2. Interview with Tina, June 2004.

*length! Plumb the depths! Rise to the heights! Live full lives, full in the fullness of God."*

As a child in Sunday School we used to sing a wonderful little song entitled *The Love of Jesus is so Wonderful.* Encouraged to do the actions as we sang, the chorus rang out,

*It's so high, you can't get over it,*

*So low, you can't get under it,*

*So wide, you can't get round it, Oh, wonderful love!'*

However, the *extravagant dimensions* of God's amazing love are not merely meant to be sung about, or talked about. Rather they are designed to be experienced. Paul wants us to "grasp" and "know" the love of God. His prayer opens for us the possibility that we can reach out to seize and possess God's love, and in the process come to experience it for ourselves. The knowledge of this love was not designed to be locked up in the pages of a book, but to be lived out each day of our lives.

*Sounds good John, so how do I get this love?*

We need to understand that we don't *get* love – we come to know it. Right now as you read this book, you are already loved by God and you cannot be any more loved than you are at this moment. God will not, cannot. love you tomorrow one fraction more than He loves you today. The amazing fact is, whether we believe in God or not, we are loved. So, it's not about getting His love, rather it is about coming to know the love which has already been poured out on us. How can we grasp and know this love?

*"...so that Christ may dwell in your hearts through faith."* (Ephesians 3:17)

Coming to Jesus through faith is the key to knowing God's love. This cannot be found in religion. Often religion is one of the greatest hindrances to truly experiencing the love of God. Rather, this points to a vibrant relationship with the Son of God

– one, which we access by letting Him be our Boss and following wherever He leads. As we walk through this door by faith, we are introduced to the *extravagant dimensions* of His mind-renewing, life-transforming, joy-giving, depression-busting, hope-filling love. We come to know things that were there all along, but which we just couldn't see. It is impossible for God to love you a little bit. We are loved, and as we begin to grasp the immensity of love's *extravagant dimensions*, we will *"... be filled to the measure of all the fullness of God."*

In trying to grasp the awesomeness of God's love, A.W. Tozer put it this way:

"God's love is measureless. It is more: it is boundless. It has no bounds because it is not a thing but a facet of the essential nature of God. His love is something he is, and because he is infinite, that love can enfold the whole created world in itself and have room for ten thousand times ten thousand worlds besides."

In seeking to know His love, which surpasses knowledge, consider for a moment four vital statistics.

**Unconditional love**

I was sitting on a long haul flight to the Philippines via Hong Kong minding my own business when God spoke. "When you arrive, a little girl will be there. I want you to love her." I was on my way to the Helga Mosey Children's home in Santiago City, in the Philippines, to visit a project my church had been heavily involved with. I knew that up to the time of my getting on the plane, only boys were in the home, yet God's word was specific: *I was to love a little girl.*

As we entered the compound of the home we were greeted

by excited workers, anxious to tell us that a new child had just been admitted – their first girl – and her name was Joyce. Keen to meet her my eyes fell on a somewhat stunted three-year-old. Malnourished, infested with lice and crippled with cerebral palsy, my heart reached out to her as if she were my own. I wanted to take her in my arms and love her, but was forbidden to do so until they had cleaned her up.

Over the next two weeks I spent many precious, life-changing moments with Joyce. I carried her around the market (which turned a few heads) and escorted her to the hospital. I lavished her with kisses, hugs and tender words. When she cried, I cried, and hers was the first face I looked for when I got back to the Home after being out on ministry. Leaving her ranks among the hardest things I have ever done in my life. For years I had locked up my tears, but now, through *the little angel in a broken body*, like a bursting damn they flooded out. Joyce is now in heaven, but her picture adorns my home among those of my family, and perhaps a little part of her lives inside me.

I went to the Philippines to preach and bless people and ended up discovering something of the unconditional love of God. He loves us full stop. No ifs, buts or ands… *He just loves us.* He doesn't love us because we are good, pretty, healthy or useful. *He just loves us.* He doesn't love us because we love Him or because we have everything in place. *He just loves us.* He doesn't love us because of what we can offer or because of our achievements. *He just loves us.*

The boys were lined up along the goal line, waiting to be picked. Being among the better footballers that day, I and another boy were asked to be captains of our teams, and so it was our duty to pick. The usual practice was to pick the best first and leave the *less talented* to the end. But that day was different. My first choice was one of the worst footballers there. Everyone stopped and looked at me, including the kid I had picked. Pointing to himself he said, "Who me? You want me?" My team lost that day. It was worth it if only to see the smiles of acceptance on the faces of boys normally left to last and to watch them play for each other as never before.

God's pointing to you, not because you're good at what you do, or because you're successful, but simply because you're special. We struggle to believe He "picks us" because He loves us. We generally get picked because we've done something that's worth being picked for. That's how we work, but not God. He loves without condition, with no strings at all, just a big fat juicy full stop at the end of the sentence.

## Unchanging love

George Matheson was engaged to be married, with a life full of promise lying ahead of him. However, tragedy struck and, through blindness, the young man's world was plunged into darkness. Worse still was to follow, for his young fiancée, who could not face a life with a blind man, abandoned him and their plans for marriage. Broken hearted, George sought solace in the love of God. In the darkness of his own pain, he penned one of the greatest hymns ever written:

*O love that wilt not let me go,*
*I rest my weary soul in Thee:*
*I give Thee back the life I owe,*
*That in Thine ocean depths its flow*
*May richer, fuller be.*[3]

---

3. *The New Redemption Hymnal*, hymn 756.

The length of God's unchanging love breathes hope into every heart that grasps the knowledge of it. To know that His love will not and cannot change towards us, brings us to a place of rest and security. When I succeed, He loves me, and when I fail, He loves me. He loved me before I had a Ph.D and He loves me now. He loves me when I'm flying high and everything I touch turns to gold. He loves me when I can't even get off the ground and dust is the best I can offer. His love does not change, although we do. We can be up and down like the proverbial yo-yo, but this is not God; this is not His love.

A Hasidic story tells of a great celebration in heaven after the Israelites were delivered from the Egyptians at the Red Sea and the Egyptian armies were drowned. The angels were cheering and dancing and everyone in heaven was full of joy. Then one of the angels asked the archangel Michael, "Where is God? Why isn't He here celebrating with us?" Michael answered, "God is not here because He is off by Himself weeping. You see, many thousands of His children were drowned today!"[4]

God can't disguise the fact that His love cannot change. Humanity has benefited from this galactic fact even though most have never appreciated it. When Jonah's message was received by the people of Nineveh the whole city turned to God. Every one of the 120,000 people responded to God's offer of mercy, yet Jonah, the man of God who had delivered the message, was furious.

He didn't like the Ninevites, he wanted them all to die, but he soon discovered God had different ideas. Jonah's response to God shows us something of the nature of God's love:

*"I knew that you are a gracious and compassionate God, slow to anger and abounding in love, a God who relents from sending calamity."* (Jonah 4:2)

4. Campolo, T., *Let Me Tell You a Story*, Word, 2000, pp.6-7.

In other words, "I knew you would do this. I know what you are like. I've tasted your love and now so have *they!*" People think Jonah ran away because he was afraid of going to Nineveh, but this is not so. Jonah ran away because he knew God's love had the power to change the city. The truth was, he wanted them all to die. The unchanging love of God was the irritation of the prophet and the salvation of the city.

### Unreserved love

During the trench warfare of World War I, a lieutenant commanded his men to sneak across a field and attack the enemy. As the men inched their way towards the enemy positions, gunfire rang out and with bullets flying in every direction the men retreated to the safety of their own trench. When the shooting stopped, everything was quiet except for the moaning of one man who had been left behind in no-man's land. The wounded soldier kept crying for his friend George, begging him to come and save him. George in turn pleaded with the young lieutenant to let him go and save his friend, but permission was refused.

"I've lost him. I don't want to lose you too."

George persisted in his request and finally, in exasperation, the lieutenant gave the order and said, "If you want to get yourself killed, go ahead! I'm tired of listening to your whining. Go out and get yourself killed, if that's what you want to do!"

George went out into the darkness and slowly dragged his friend back to the trench. The two men collapsed in a heap in the trench, George exhausted from the ordeal. Unfortunately, his friend was dead. The lieutenant yelled, "George, I told you there was no point to your bravery. Why did you risk your life? You put the entire unit in jeopardy. And for what? There was no point to what you did. You were a fool!" George answered, "I was no fool. When I got to him he was still alive and the last words he said were, 'George! I knew you'd come!'"[5]

Love will do whatever needs to be done in order to achieve its goal. Humanity will never understand what God did to demonstrate His love for the world. The stark summation that Jesus came, lived and died does not even begin to calculate what it cost heaven to do what it did. Paul tries to sum it up when he writes,

*"Who, being in very nature God, did not consider equality with God something to be grasped, but made Himself nothing, taking the very nature of a servant, being made in human likeness. And being found in appearance as a man, He humbled Himself And became obedient to death – even death on a cross!"* (Philippians 2:6-8)

The height of God's unreserved love is witnessed in the depth to which He was prepared to stoop to save humanity and the world. These few verses demonstrate the abandonment of reserve and the extreme measures God took so that we could grasp and know His love. When Jesus walked the earth, He was often criticised by the religious people, especially for the way He mixed and mingled with sinner-types. On one occasion they said of Jesus, *"This man welcomes sinners, and eats with them"* (Luke 15:2). This was meant as a criticism, but Jesus accepted it as a compliment. Jesus expressed the unreservedness of God's love when touching lepers, teaching women, associating with government sympathisers and healing people, even on the Sabbath.

The height of the love of God is immense. The Son of God got off His throne, let go of every right and privilege that was His and

5. Campolo, *Story*, op.cit., pp.17-18.

came to earth, for one reason and one reason only... because He loved you!

## Unlimited love

A little girl stayed for dinner at the home of her school friend and among the vegetables was a bowl of sprouts. The mother asked the girl if she liked sprouts. The child replied very politely, "Oh yes, I love them." When the bowl of sprouts was passed around she declined to take any. Her friend's mother said, "I thought you said you loved sprouts?" The girl replied sweetly, "Oh yes, I do, but not enough to eat them!"

Do you know what a limit is?

A limit is a boundary line, a terminal point; a line which may not or cannot be passed. But when it comes to love, God has no limits. There is no-one He can't love and there is no situation His love cannot invade. There are no limits on God's love for us. The big problem is that *we* place limits on His love. *We* decide who He can or cannot love; what He can or cannot do.

Jesus was walking through a city one day surrounded by thousands of people. At the height of His public popularity, the crowds were pulling and pushing, trying to get close to the miracle-laden prophet from Galilee. In the midst of the noise and with the air heavy with expectation, Jesus suddenly stopped. He looked up into a sycamore tree and spoke to a man who had gained a good view of the procession, while perched in the branches. "Zacchaeus, come down immediately. I must stay at your house today." Zacchaeus was a tax-collector – a hard enough job at the best of times, but when the job also meant sympathy with the Roman occupying force and the wholesale exploitation and over-charging of the people, you can see why he was never invited out much. The people hated him. He was bad news and his house crossed the boundary line of decency. Such a man was firmly off-limits. It stands to reason, then, that the Son of God would go to his house for tea! By the end of that day, Zacchaeus was giving half his possessions to the poor and paying back anyone he had cheated up to four times the amount. Jesus was able to say, *"Today salvation has come to this house..."* (Luke 19:9). The only reason salvation got the chance to come to the house of the vertically challenged tax-collector was because Jesus crossed the line and went where no religious man had gone before.

God's love is like that. The reach of His love knows no boundaries and its depths no limits at all. He will go where He has to go to touch those who need His love. Ironically, the minute we start to put limits on God's love, the moment we decide who can or cannot be loved, is when God will show up in a procession and blow the little box we're trying to put Him in to hell and beyond.

Peter was having a nap one day when God gave him a rude awakening. In his dream, a large sheet was lowered in front of him containing all sorts of unclean animals that good Jewish boys would never touch, let alone eat. To his horror, God suggested that Peter have a barbecue and tuck into the once forbidden menu. Peter refused to eat and God spoke:

*"Do not call anything impure that God has made clean."*

After the third repeat of the dream, someone came to the door of the house where Peter was staying. They had been sent by a God-fearing Roman Gentile named Cornelius, who, they claimed, had been told by a holy angel to send for Peter! "Aren't Gentiles off limits... especially Roman ones?"

Do you think you are off-limits to the love of God? I have met people over the years who are convinced that God no longer loves them, and even if He could, He really should not. Failure, disappointment and pain have all conspired to help build a large fence carrying the sign, "Trespassers will be prosecuted... and if you're reading this God, don't even think about climbing over my fence!"

Did you know you are *not* off limits to God? Did you know you *can* be forgiven? Did you know you *can* receive a fresh knowledge of God's love for *you* – a love which has never changed or gone away?

Read this description of love and see if it can't touch you or the people around you:

*"Love is patient, love is kind. It does not envy, it does not boast, it is not proud.*

*It is not rude, it is not self-seeking, it is not easily angered, it keeps no record of wrongs.*

*Love does not delight in evil but rejoices with the truth. Love always protects, always trusts, always hopes, always perseveres. Love never fails."*

(1 Corinthians 13:4-8)

Take a moment to grasp and know the vital statistics of God's incredible love. See its width, length, height and depth and understand that God wants to lavish all that on you. This love was not intended for theological books but for your life. God's desire is that you will know His love in such a way that it is woven into every aspect of your life. There is nothing you can do to make God love you more! There is nothing you can do to make God love you less! The *extravagant dimensions* of His love are unconditional, unchanging, unreserved and unlimited, and it is for *you!*

# Chapter 3
## Jesus Loves Me This I Know

"Love is the only rational act."[1]

The following advert appeared in the East African Standard: "Nanyuki farmer seeks lady with tractor with view to companionship and possible marriage. *Send picture of tractor.*"[2] There's nothing like being practical I suppose and in some ways I do admire the honesty of the chap. For the Western mindset with its sentimentalised approach to love, relationships and marriage, this seems a bit ... mercenary! After all, love is love and we would all like to believe you can't really put a price on that.

In 1993 a movie was released which caused some controversy, not because of the extreme violence, excessive bad language or gratuitous sex, but because of the "business agreement" at the heart of the plot. David and Diana Murphy were a young couple very much in love. He was an architect and she was a real estate agent. They'd found the perfect spot to build their dream home and borrowed to finance the project.

---

1. Albom, M., Tuesdays with Morrie, USA, 1997, p.52.
2. Gammons, P., *All Preachers Great & Small*, 1989, p.33. My italics.

When the recession hit they stood to lose everything they owned, so in one final, desperate effort to keep their dream alive they went to Las Vegas to try and win the money they needed. After a disastrous day at the tables, they were broke and without hope. Enter John Gage, a super millionaire, played by Robert Redford. Captivated by the beauty of Diana, he made them an *Indecent Proposal* and offered David $1 million for one night of sex with his wife. Gage was certain that every man could be bought and that everyone and everything had a price, even love! Cynical, I know, but was he right?

It was just a movie, however, two years earlier a book was released which shocked America. It was entitled *The Day America Told the Truth*. In a national survey, one of the questions asked was, "What would you do in exchange for $10 million?" Of those questioned, two-thirds agreed to at least one of the following and some agreed to several.

- 3% would put their children up for adoption
- 4% would have a sex-change operation
- 6% would change race
- 7% would kill a stranger
- 16% would leave their spouse
- 16% would give up their American citizenship
- 23% would become a prostitute for a week or more
- 25% would abandon their family
- 25% would leave their church[3]

The same questions were asked in regard to sums of $5 million,

---

3. Patterson, J., & Kim, P., *The Day America Told the Truth*, New York, 1991, pp.65-66.

$4 million and $3 million and the results remained pretty much the same. It was only at $2 million where interviewers began to see a fall-off in what people were willing to do!

I know *you* wouldn't do anything like this, but it seems there are many out there who would at least be tempted to do the unthinkable if the price was right. As someone said, "The average person in our society prostitutes their decency, their creativity, their morality, and their autonomy so that they can make a living. Prostituting your body once for a million dollars is just doing the same damn thing, only it's more honest. Not to mention more profitable."[4]

*What price love?*

Let's consider for a moment what price was paid for us in the name of love. The Bible is clear: God loved the world and He passionately loves us, but as we look deeper, the story becomes even more amazing.

*"But God demonstrates His own love for us in this: While we were still sinners, Christ died for us."* (Romans 5:8)

This incredible statement represents the immensity of God's love in many ways. It shows us His love was not just theoretical but proactively practical. He demonstrated His love to us even before we had any thought or consideration of Him. We didn't make the first move, He did. Such was the extent of God's love that Jesus came to a world that was largely oblivious of Him and lavished on it the best that heaven had to offer.

*"This is how God showed His love among us: He sent His one and only Son into the world that we might live through Him."* (1 John 4:9)

---

4. Film Unlimited website message board for the movie *Indecent Proposal*. This was left in answer to the question, "Would you do it?" (16th July 2004).

God knew exactly how much loving us would cost and was prepared to put His money where His mouth was and pay whatever price had to be paid. He didn't look around heaven for a broken down, no-one will miss him if he's gone, angel. Instead He looked for the best heaven could give. He calculated the most heaven could afford and without hesitation He paid it, for us!

*"This is love: not that we loved God, but that He loved us and sent His Son as an atoning sacrifice for our sins."* (1 John 4:10)

Ben Potts was only fourteen years old when he first dabbled in drugs, but from then there was a gradual progression into horror for him and his family. On a weekend in Amsterdam, he was introduced to heroin and crack cocaine and, in his own words, "Things went downhill rapidly." To feed the habit Ben would beg, steal or borrow money from anyone. "I don't care who I steal off, I have one thing on my mind and that's crack and heroin. My nan… my granddad… anyone who came in contact with me, anyone who came close to me… were gonna' get robbed."

Ben's mum, Nicky, a college lecturer, continued to stand by him as he spiralled out of control. Soon, however, Ben was sleeping in the garden shed, wrapping himself in brown paper bags, a danger to himself and others. Advised to kick him out and cut him off, Nicky refused to let go and continued to believe that her son could turn the corner and beat the habit. In the years that followed Ben frequented many prisons for various offences. Later, destitute and on the streets, he described the humiliation of his experience as he was kicked out of doorways like a dog. "My self-esteem, my self-respect was on the floor." He returned home one morning at 1.00am, wet through and freezing cold. As his mother looked at him, love took over and she reached out, got hold of him, hugged him and wanted to make everything right. He slept at home for the first time in years that night and Nicky went to bed knowing that for once, all her children were safe. Ben is now on a detox programme, hoping to stay clean and make a new life.[5]

When Jesus wanted to illustrate the value of humanity and the immensity of God's love, He used a similar picture. The boy in question wasn't a *druggie*, but was penniless, hungry and covered in the stench of shame and failure. He had blown his inheritance and was returning home hoping for a bed in the servants' quarters. He reckoned that's all he deserved and that's all he was worth. But he did not reckon on one thing: the power of love! Waiting for him was a father who anxiously scanned the horizon for the silhouette of his precious son. On the day his son returned, the father didn't walk out to meet him, *he ran.* He didn't fold his arms in judgement, *he hugged.* He didn't criticise, *he kissed.* He didn't punish his son that day, *he blessed him!*[6] Those privileged enough to hear Jesus' story that day got more than entertainment. Through the words of the Master they heard the heartbeat of heaven and caught a glimpse of a world pregnant with mercy, grace and love – virtues which were painfully absent from a religion heavy with rules and laced with self-righteousness, as reflected in the reaction of the son's older brother.

*What price love?*

Anna Warner wrote a hymn which over the years has become a children's song. It was originally written with four verses and a chorus, though if you've ever heard or sung this song, it will probably only have been the first verse and chorus:

*Jesus loves me! This I know, for the Bible tells me so*
*Little ones to Him belong, they are weak, but He is strong*

---

5. My Story – *It's All Down to Ben*, broadcast on Radio 4, 15/07/04.
6. Why not read the story for yourself, Luke 15:11-32.

*Yes, Jesus loves me, yes, Jesus loves me*
*Yes, Jesus loves me, the Bible tells me so*

The second verse reads,

*Jesus loves me! He who died, heaven's gate to open wide*
*He will wash away my sin, let this little child come in*

Do *you* know He loves you?

What exactly do *you* know?

*"I praise you because I am fearfully and wonderfully made; Your works are wonderful, **I know that full well**."* (Psalm 139:14)

We could fill a whole book on being fearfully and wonderfully made, but it's the last phrase I want to pick up on for a moment. "I know that full well." David *knew* that he was made a certain way, *he knew* who had made him, and *he knew* that God's works were incredible. His life was buoyant and blessed as a consequence of that which *he knew*.

**The knowledge**

When you get into a taxi in London, you hope the driver knows his way around the congested city, especially at the prices they charge. When you say, "Take me to Westminster Chapel please" you don't want to hear, "Where's that then?" The only way cabbies can prove they know their way around London is by taking an exam called "The Knowledge". It can be learned at schools set up just to prepare future taxi drivers. On average, students spend 3 hours a day studying the London map and another 3 hours riding a motorcycle to get acquainted with the routes and streets of the city. It takes most students more than a year to prepare for The

Knowledge if they study full-time. "It's an intimate knowledge of the streets of London … that's really all it is," explained examiner Rodney Stentiford. "Getting to know all the streets and everything of interest in London. Anywhere a passenger might want to be taken to."[7]

Their knowledge determines where they go and how they drive. Their knowledge could mean the difference between a twenty-minute ride and a frustrating one hour twenty minute detour, not to mention the extra expense! Next time you get into a London taxi, ask the driver if he has The Knowledge. If he hasn't, you might want to find another cab.

What you know will determine how you live and the direction you take your life. The knowledge of the love of God in our lives will radically impact our approach to living and influence every decision we make. Without that knowledge, we may find ourselves driving up dead-end streets, travelling down a one-way system the wrong way, or getting completely lost. We can stick our finger in the air and hope that we make it, or we can rely on the knowledge and advice of others to direct us to where we need to go, but all of that is a risky business. I always think it is better to know; to have a map to hand and to be able to plot your own course.

When we know we are loved, when we can sing the simple song, "Jesus loves me this I *know*" and mean it, then we have the power to plot our own course and find the route which God has mapped out for us. He wants us to have The Knowledge of His love.

## Check the attic

Have you ever heard of a 19th Century American painter called

---

7. CNN.com, Travel guide news, 16/07/04.

Martin Johnson Heade? If that name rings a bell, and you think you've got one of his paintings tucked away in your attic, you might want to read on. One of his landscape paintings depicting the North Shore of New England, still in its original gilded frame, in virtually untouched condition, was found in a Boston, Massachusetts attic by its owner, who had no idea of its worth. Auctioneer, John McInnis found the painting leaning against an attic rafter and persuaded the owner to take it to auction. On the 7th December 2003, the painting that had gathered dust in an attic for sixty years was sold for $1,006,250.

*Do you know what you've got?* Do you know what wealth and riches have been placed into your hands and into your life?

Many live unaware of what they have in their attic. They live impoverished lives because they live outside of the knowledge of God's love for them and to them. They refuse to take God's Word that they are loved and so continue to live on the poverty line, when a million dollar treasure is within their possession – they just don't know it. How many are unaware that God's love is in their house? How many live outside of the knowledge of things that may be right in front of them? How many are attending church, but only engage with powerless religion and miss the God of love, unaware that a treasure lies within?

When we know we are loved, when we can sing "Jesus loves me this *I know*" and mean it, it opens the door for us to experience a quality of life far above the mediocrity of poverty and the limitation of ignorance. Many live on the crumbs of "I hope Jesus loves me", "I think Jesus loves me" or "If I'm good Jesus will love me." Yet, there is for you the wealth that comes from knowing for sure that we are loved. Now would be a good time to take an inventory of your life. Why live in poverty when there's a masterpiece sitting in your attic?

## Don't be a donkey

Some friends of mine bought me a book entitled, *Eeyore's Little Book of Gloom*. The back cover reads, "A leaden collection of Pessimistic Ponderings from the 100 Acre Wood's resident cynic. Perfect for those who are tired of Life or tedious little tomes full of Joy." For those of you who know the Winnie the Pooh stories written by A.A. Milne, you will know that Eeyore is dominated by a negative outlook on life and usually his feelings rule his reactions. His droopy ears, sad eyes and pinned-on tail all add to the blueness of his existence. That and the fact that he is after all a blue donkey!

Some of the things Eeyore comes out with are positively depressing (did I just do an oxymoron?) and if these are an expression of what he truly believes, it's no wonder the lad is struggling. Let me give you a sample:

*"Invisible Mending,*

You can give a donkey a happy ending… but the miserable beginning remains forever."

*"Gaze on Greyness,*

Cultivate a permanently tragic expression by staring at your reflection for hours on end; it's sure to bring a touch of gloom to even the sunniest of days."

*"Expect the worst,*

Even if someone remembers to come to your birthday party, they will almost certainly eat your present on the way… or break it!"

And finally,

"Things can only get wetter!"[8]

---

8. *Eeyore's Little Book of Gloom*, 1999, inspired by A.A.Milne and E.H.Shepard.

Poor old Eeyore, what can be done for him? Surrounded by friends who love him and the wonders of the 100 Acre Wood, he can see only the grey side of life, convinced that every silver lining has a cloud! Yet this is what happens when we allow our feelings to govern our belief system and thinking: "Jesus doesn't love me, He couldn't love me ... why would He love me?" When our feelings are king, truth gets pushed to the fringes of our minds and sometimes banished completely. When feelings reign, we are at the mercy of the weather, the news reports, our hormones or a million other things that might touch our emotional scale.

Have you ever noticed that one of the first questions we often ask people is, "How are you feeling?" Automatically we focus our attention on how *we feel* instead of what *we know*. So the conversation begins negatively or positively, not because of truth, but because of how we happen to feel at that moment. If I went on how I felt, I'd pray twice a year, read my Bible once a month and only give my wealth away when moved to do it. Surely our lives must be governed by something more than how we feel? Surely our understanding of God's love must rise above the level of our emotions? If we are to be people of influence, successfully engaging with the world, we've got to move beyond *Eeyore's Little Book of Gloom* and get to the truth; get to what we know!

Jesus loves me, this *I know*!

**What others think they know**

When we don't know, we are at the mercy of what others know. When we don't know what we think then we are forever influenced by what others think. In some instances, knowledge really *is* power. In 2004, the United States of America and Britain went to war with Iraq under the premise that Iraq had weapons of mass destruction and that within forty-five minutes they could be operational. The intelligence services were certain they had the correct information, and so on the basis of what a few people claimed to know, war was declared! Armies engaged, Saddam Hussein was toppled and Baghdad was taken. But we're still searching for the weapons. I do not want to debate the rights and wrongs of war in this chapter, but I do want to point out to you the power of knowing something (or not) in an arena where others are not sure.

When we don't know, then how do we determine the difference between wrong information and misinformation? What's the difference between truth, fake news and propaganda? The fact is, when we don't know, we are dependent on others to tell us and therefore at the mercy of what they think they know – regardless of whether they are right or wrong.

I remember preparing myself for a minor medical operation. The date was set and I was ready! It was at this point that I decided to ask other people who had been through the operation what their experiences were and to ask if they could give me any advice. That was a big mistake. Everyone had a different opinion because they all had different experiences. Some were good and others were positively horrific. Depending on who I talked to determined my future. I would either be back to work the next day with a smile on my face, or I'd be permanently walking like John Wayne after a looonnngggg horse ride! Their knowledge was now dictating my feelings. I was held captive by the things other people knew, whether true or not. Having been there and done it ... I now *know* for myself!

If we know Jesus loves us, then we are not at the mercy of another's knowledge. If we know we are loved by the God of love, then a theological expert can walk into the room and not sway us. If we know God's love, even the father of lies can't get his claws on us, ever! Once we know the simple, life-changing piece of knowledge that Jesus loves us, it can and will revolutionise us forever.

Eeyore once said.

"Nobody minds. Nobody cares.

Pathetic, that's what it is."[9]

*No Eeyore, you are wrong!*

*Jesus minds. Jesus cares.*

*Love, that's what it is!*

9. *Book of Gloom*, op.cit.

# Chapter 4
# Nothing to Prove

"By instinct I feel I must do something in order to be accepted."[1]

As I looked around the room it seemed to me that all the other young men were as nervous as I was. The shuffling feet, well-chewed nails and beads of perspiration gave it away. We were in the Castlereagh Police Station in Belfast. No, not waiting for sentencing, we were there for an interrogation of a different kind. The Royal Ulster Constabulary (now the Northern Ireland Police Service), were recruiting for their Cadet Academy. Over 650 boys had applied and with only 25 places up for grabs it was going to be an interesting day. A basic medical and a tough entrance exam were waiting for us through the locked double doors. As I glanced through the glass panels in the doors, I could see row upon row of chairs and tables and a police officer slowly placing papers on each desk. As a teenager I was *sure* this was what I wanted to do for the rest of my life and I was fairly confident that I'd make it. A friend of our family who was a member of the police force had told my Dad, "John is the type of young man we're after. He will have no problem getting in."

1. Yancy, P., *What's So Amazing About Grace*, Zondervan, 1997, p.71.

I survived the day, flying through the basic medical and passing the exam, but it was the second medical, which was my undoing. They found a weakness in my left eye, which meant my eyesight wasn't perfect. Everything else was fine and in good working order, except my slightly weak left eye. I wasn't blind, just a little challenged. Surely it wasn't that bad? My protests fell on deaf ears, however, and I had to endure the, "We think you are great, but..." speech. I was told to apply again when I was eighteen. "You're the type of young man we're after. You will have no problem getting in." I was sure I'd heard that before somewhere! Twenty-five were accepted that day, but I wasn't one of them. I just was not good enough; not quite what they wanted. Application denied!

To approve someone or something is to pronounce or think them "good"; to have a favourable opinion of them.[2] Today, millions of people all over our planet are seeking approval from husbands, wives, parents, children, their boss at work or even God! For most, if not all, of these people, this will be sought in the context of doing something to "earn" the approval of that significant other. The lengths to which people are willing to go to get the approval they crave is amazing and sometimes tragic. Most people I know have been raised under the merciless taskmaster of working for approval, but the Bible teaches us that there is an alternative.

When it came to the piano, David Helfgott was a child prodigy. His father, an immigrant to Australia from war-torn Europe, wanted David to succeed and drove the boy relentlessly in his quest for perfection. No performance was ever quite good enough and David, who longed for the approval of his father, sought to match the expectations of his father by doing what was asked of him.

---

2. Oxford Dictionary.

David moved to London to study music and while there suffered a horrific mental breakdown. He returned to an institution in Australia and after many years was released into the community. The 1996 movie *Shine* graphically depicts this period of David's life. Alone, strange, dirty and unable to relate to anyone, he longed for approval. One rainy evening he entered a restaurant because he saw it had a piano. His hair was long and matted, his clothes soaked and smelly, and a limp and rather pathetic cigarette hung from his mouth. As he made his way to the piano, everyone stopped talking and looked with disdain on the intruder. David sat down and touched a few keys randomly, which provoked some laughter and a little abuse.

"Play something for us" he was asked, and play he did. David launched into a rendition of the *Minute Waltz*, which stunned and amazed all present. While he played he held them spellbound, gripped by his genius. As the applause rang out to shouts of "Bravo" David was now accepted and approved. Moments before he had been a dirty, filthy tramp off the streets. His piano playing had earned him approval. He was now pronounced "good" and those present had a favourable opinion of him. Thank God for the piano!

This is how most of us live and this is how many people relate to God. We are more at ease with the idea of earning the love of God and doing something to get His approval, than with the truth that we are loved, approved and accepted by God, regardless of what we can or cannot do. If God set a test we'd never pass it. If He set the standards none of us would have a hope of reaching them in order to get His approval – His benchmark is way too high for us. Yet we still comfort ourselves with the thought that, somehow, what we do contributes to our standing with Him and gives us the right to receive all He has for us.

Read these words carefully:

*"How great is the love the Father has lavished on us, that we should be called children of God! And that is what we are!"* (1 John 3:1)

God has lavished His great love on us, *"that we should be called..."* The amazing fact is that heaven's love was poured out onto our lives *before* we were children of God. *Before* we could have done anything to earn His love. Even before we were aware that He loved us in the first place. His love was given and we were approved! So why, having now been accepted by God through the outpouring of His love, do we spend so much time trying to work for His approval?

Martin Luther was known to spend up to six hours in the confessional. Penance was the order of the day and Luther, a deeply devout man, wanted to get close to God and know His love. His ambition was to do whatever he needed to do in order to be approved by God. However, one day in the midst of his pursuit, he had a revelation of the truth: "The just shall live by faith." On receiving that revelation he wrote one word in the margin of his Bible beside that verse. That word was "Alone!" He'd discovered that he could receive from God by *faith alone* everything he had sought to earn through works. This simple truth transformed his life and the face of Christendom.

How easy it sounds, but how hard it can be. As a young person growing up in Belfast, I would often look down my nose at "those poor Roman Catholics" as they tried to earn salvation and the love of God through Hail Marys, confession, penance and mass. They were in darkness and *we Protestants* had the truth. Yet, the truth of my experience was, although I believed in the life of faith in my head, the reality of my lifestyle pointed to my own form of *Protestant penance*. I would fast and pray because I thought this made God like me more. I would confess the same sins over and over again until *I felt* that I was forgiven and it had been dealt with. I might as well have been saying my Hail Mary, confessing to the priest or making a pilgrimage to Rome. Different team, same mentality! I was justified by faith, but in reality helped by a liberal dose of good works, just as a backup in case the faith thing didn't work. The result was horrific for me.

As a child we sang the nursery rhyme.

*The grand old Duke of York, he had 10,000 men, he marched them up to the top of the hill and he marched them down again. When they were up they were up, and when they were down they were down, and when they were only half way up, they were neither up nor down.*

This was my spiritual experience. If I had a good week, living well, getting victory over lust, not losing my temper, sticking to my Bible reading programme and notching up a few extra minutes on my prayer time-sheet... then all was well with the world. God and I were pals, life was great and I was a spiritual giant, loved by God. However, if I had a bad week, then God hated me, I was worthy only of hell and I could not take Communion in case I died! People put it down to me being a teenager, but it was much more serious than that. I had no clue how the love of God really worked. I was still in "earning mode", when I had already been loved and approved by heaven!

As a boy, I was a member of the Boys' Brigade and loved it. Every week I would be with my friends and we would march, drill, carry flags, learn, play football, annoy our captain and generally enjoy ourselves. Each year we had a display to which parents, family and friends were invited. It was the high point of our year and something we all worked towards. On the night of the display we would demonstrate our year's development through sketches, gymnastics and marching skills. There were also presentations awarded for badge work, promotions and for those who had won competitions. The most coveted awards were Footballer of the Year, the Scripture Cup, and one for the Best Overall Boy in the company. As we stood in ranks looking at the trophies, boys, parents and friends would hold their breath waiting to see who had won these awards. "The winner is…"

The sense of approval when your name was called and you stepped forward with the applause of all those you loved ringing in your ears was immeasurable.

Feeling approved can be intoxicating and addictive. Once tasted, we like it and we will do whatever is needed to ensure we keep enjoying it. The problem is, the approval we crave can be built on the wrong foundation and measured by the wrong criteria. Over the years in church ministry, I have seen wonderful people fall into this vicious trap. They measure themselves in terms of their doing and expect the approval of others and even of God on the same basis. Their worth is wrapped up in their doing. The more they do, the more important they are and the more approved they feel. The big problem with this belief system is that it is never satisfied. It will always need more, it will demand things we can no longer give and it will leave us empty, broken and disillusioned. The life-changing truth confronts us again: God loves us and we are already approved!

There are many enemies to living in the approval of God's love, but two in particular keep raising their ugly heads. The first is **insecurity**. In the verse that we read earlier, John not only tells us that we can be called children of God, but confidently concludes, "And that is what we are!" If we don't know we are children of

God, and if we're not secure in the reality of that, then we will forever be working to be approved by a Father who already loves us. If we are not sure, then this will either drive us away from the presence of God or into a lifestyle dominated by the need for approval and assurance.

The second enemy, which feeds the first, is **ignorance**. When we don't know who we are, what we've been given and what sort of love we're dealing with, then we will never enjoy the full life that such love can bring. In this verse John proclaims, "How great is the love..." Another version of the verse puts it, "Behold what manner of love..." The idea is that we stop, take a look, get to grips with and understand just what sort of love we are actually dealing with. This is no ordinary love – this is the love of God, His own brand of love, which once given cannot be taken back. If we don't know we are loved or just how much we are loved, then we'll live in the darkness of ignorance and forever seek the approval of a God who has already loved and approved us.

When Jesus came to earth, He came to demonstrate the love of God. He needed to find a way of doing that which would register with all of humanity. Ultimately, He died for the sin of the world, a story we know so well. But before that, He chose to share His life with a bunch of young men, so diverse and unusual they would have been the last choice for anyone serious about world domination. Jesus had many followers, but the Bible teaches us He specifically called twelve young men to "be *with* Him". They would get up close and personal with God in flesh. They would get to hear first hand the words of God from the Word Himself. They would see miracles that would beggar belief. But most of all, they would experience the love of God as He intended it.

Loved, approved and called, their journeys have something to say to us today. To help us understand something of the immensity of the love we're dealing with, I wish to draw on the experience of just three of them.

### The love of Jesus accepted *Judas*

I do not wish to get into a deep theological debate about whether Judas was "saved" or not, but I do want to make one incontrovertible statement: Judas was loved, and because he was loved, he was accepted by Jesus. If we did not know what Judas was up to, we would never have known by the way Jesus treated him. Jesus clearly knew some stuff about him, but He chose to love and accept him as one of the twelve.

The evidence shows that Jesus knew Judas was (in the words of Jesus Himself) a devil (John 6:70-71); that he was stealing from the group money bag (John 12:4-6); and that he had set his heart on betrayal (John 13:27). Yet do you ever hear Jesus single him out for attention? Apart from the confrontation over the woman who broke the alabaster box over Jesus, we never see Jesus put him down. Does Jesus ever threaten him or kick him out?

Some might say, "Well, the reason Jesus didn't expose him was because Judas was the betrayer and this was a means to an end." In other words, Jesus put up with Judas because he was the one to do the dirty deed, not because He loved him. But Jesus didn't *use* Judas, He loved him. Jesus didn't *put up with* Judas, He loved him. The very night Judas went out and betrayed Jesus, the Master stooped and washed the feet of His friend. Judas must have witnessed this act of unrestrained love and been touched by its depth and grace. Whatever Judas did that night, he did for himself, not because he was unloved!

This is how we are loved. God has never been disillusioned with us because He never had any illusions in the first place. He knows all about us yet still loves us. His love allows Him to approve and accept us, even when there are things still in our heart that He wishes weren't there. Our acceptance by God has nothing to do with a means to an end plan in the back of His mind. It has little to do with anything we have achieved or any position we hold. It has absolutely nothing to do with our upbringing, the colour of our skin or our nationality. We are accepted for no other reason than that we are loved!

I remember sitting with someone in Her Majesty's Prison, Wakefield. Around the same age as me, he had spent nearly a third of his life in prison. I explained to him about the love of God and how he could experience it. I will never forget his answer. It rings in my ears, even today.

"It can't be that easy. There must be a catch. What is it?"

The truth is, the love of Jesus is that simple, for there is no agenda, only love. There is no motivation, only love. The only reason you and I are accepted, given the right to be called children of God, is because we are loved.

## The love of Jesus allowed *Thomas* to be himself

Thomas has been given the nickname, *Doubting Thomas*, because of his refusal to accept that Jesus had risen from the dead.

*"Unless I see the nail marks in his hands and put my finger where the nails were, and put my hand into his side, I will not believe it."* (John 20:25)

This was not the first time Thomas had expressed concern at Jesus' actions and teachings. When Jesus indicated that He was going to go to Lazarus, Thomas "comforted" the group with the words,

*"Let us also go, that we may die with Him."* (John 11:16)

Later, in the last week of His life, when Jesus was explaining things to His followers, Thomas questioned: *"Lord, we don't know where you are going, so how can we know the way?"* (John 14:5)

The love of Jesus was such that it allowed Thomas to be himself. Thomas was comfortable enough around Jesus to express his opinions because of the level of acceptance he felt. Even though some of Thomas' opinions were not very helpful, Jesus nonetheless allowed him to express them and did not put him down for them.

When Billy Graham preached, the hymn *Just as I am* would often be sung by the choir as people made their way to the front.

*Just as I am, without one plea,*
*But that Thy blood was shed for me,*
*And that Thou bidst me come to Thee,*
*O Lamb of God, I come.*

The last of the seven verses says this:
*Just as I am, of that free love*
*The breadth, length, depth and height to prove,*
*Here for a season, then above,*
*O Lamb of God, I come.*[3]

It sounds great, but in reality the practice can be very much different. God may not have a problem for us to come as we are, but the challenge arises for those who claim to follow God: do we allow people to truly come as they are to receive the love of God, giving them time to make a journey?

Don't get me wrong, I'm into discipleship and the challenge of change, but it is interesting that Jesus, our great model on how to do things, let His followers make a journey with Him over a

---

3. Written by Charlotte Elliott.

period of three years, and in that time, allowed them to be and express themselves as they were. Religion, whatever the label and however it is expressed, demands conformity and uniformity. It stifles individuality and squashes any form of opposition. Religion fears difference and so, through rules, dress code and culture, it seeks to control and clone those under its influence. Jesus wasn't into that, because that is not the love of God. He allowed His followers to be themselves. They were not given uniforms or a demand for uniformity; rather He presented to them His claims and asked them to connect to them at whatever stage of the journey they were at.

One of the things I love about Church is its wondrous diversity. God didn't make us the same, so why should that change in the Church? The understanding that we are loved brings us to the freedom to be ourselves. Our journey will require change and alteration, but only from a position of love and acceptance. Lifestyle change must come from the power of truth, not the dictates of a crowd.

Did Thomas change?

Tradition tells us that the doubter walked half way across the world to share the good news of the resurrected Christ, eventually dying a martyr's death on a hill, just outside Madras in India. Allowed to be himself, even in doubt, he encountered the love of Jesus and changed forever.

**The love of Jesus assisted *John* to become the Apostle of love**
When we read the wonderful words of John in his letters to the Church, we are amazed and blessed.

*"Dear friends, since God so loved us, we also ought to love one another."* (1 John 4:11)

*"If anyone says, 'I love God,' yet hates his brother, he is a liar. For anyone who does not love his brother, whom he has seen, cannot love God, whom he has not seen."* (1 John 4:20)

Now listen to these words,

*"Lord, do you want us to call fire down from heaven to destroy them?"* (Luke 9:54)

(Try saying that with an Irish accent, it really works).

Both words were spoken by the same person! John and his brother James were given the nicknames *Sons of Thunder* by Jesus. Now we know why! John was reacting to the opposition from some of the Samaritans, so he said what any self-respecting Jewish boy of his day would have said: "Let's kill them, squash them into the ground, make them pay!" What a hothead! At this point I would have pulled Jesus to one side and asked, "Are you sure this kid is the type you want hanging around you? I mean the message of love and forgiveness doesn't seem to be high on his agenda. I'm not sure he has a future in the Church, Jesus!" Thankfully, I wasn't there, and even if I had been, Jesus would have given me one of those looks that said, "Button it, Andrews!" The *Thunder Boys* continued to rattle and Jesus continued to love. Later we see John reclining next to Jesus, putting his head on the Master's chest. As he recalled those moments in years to come, he would remember how he could hear the very heartbeat of God.

John was loved by Jesus. That love accepted the young hothead allowing him to be himself, even when that was rather distasteful, and assisted him to become known affectionately as the *Apostle of Love*. Time didn't change John. Pressure didn't do it, nor did his friends. Rather, it was being exposed to heaven's brand of love, which began the journey of transformation from son of thunder to Apostle of love. Out of acceptance and approval he changed; such is the power of God's love.

The story is told of a man who set out to adopt a troubled teenage girl. The girl was destructive, disobedient and dishonest and people questioned the father's logic in doing what he was doing. One day the girl came home from school and ransacked the house looking for money. By the time the father arrived home, she was gone and the house was in a mess. Upon hearing of her actions, friends urged him not to finalise the adoption. "Let her go," they said. "After all, she's not really your daughter." His response was simple yet profound: "Yes, I know. But I told her she was!"[4]

We are loved by God and because of that love *we are approved.* Having been approved we have nothing to prove. If we have nothing to prove we can just get on and live well. If we live well, knowing that we are loved, our lives will be the greatest advert for the Kingdom of God possible. We may feel by instinct that we must do something to be accepted, but the love of God says we need do nothing. Heaven screams out, "*You* are loved and you have *nothing to prove!*"

---

4. Lucado, M., *In the Grip of His Grace*, Word, 1996, p.97.

# Chapter 5
# Forgiven

"There are few joys in life like being wanted, chosen, embraced. There are few pains like being excluded, rejected, left out."[1]

Mention the name Hercules and images of a muscle-bound superhero, half-man, half-god spring to mind. His exploits in Greek mythology are legendary, standing out as one of the best known demi-gods, which is a bit of an achievement when we consider how many there were! However, I confess, I knew very little about the life of Hercules until my son Simeon (seven, at the time) read to me about the ancient hero from one of his school books. The story centred around the need for Hercules to find forgiveness for a terrible crime he had committed. The legend tells us he eventually married a lady called Megera and together they had three handsome sons. Life was good and everyone was happy. But the goddess Hera was jealous of Hercules and under the influence of one of her spells he killed his three sons. Guilty and remorseful, he ran to the temple and the priestess told him to go and see King Eurystheus who would give him twelve tasks. "If you do them all," she told him, "the gods will forgive you."

---

1. Ortberg, J., *Everybody's Normal Till You Get to Know Them*, USA, 2003, p.186.

Desperate for forgiveness, Hercules went to see the king and received his tasks. The absolution of his sins from the gods would cost him dearly.

His first task was to kill a ravenous lion that was terrorising the king. His second task was to find and kill the dreaded Hydra, a nine-headed monster whose poison was so deadly that one sniff could kill. Number three involved bringing the stag with the golden antlers to the king, followed by task four, catching a wild boar! Next he had to clean the stables of King Augeas in a day. Compared to the others this seems quite simple, until we discover that the stables hadn't been cleaned in over thirty years! On completion of task five, he had to go and kill a vicious flock of birds that would rip animals to pieces and were known to eat people. From there he was off to Crete to capture the Great White Bull. With its fire-breathing nostrils it was wrecking the island and killing many people (are you tired yet?) Task eight involved bringing back the horses of Diomedes, known for liking human flesh. Hercules had to kill Diomedes to get the beasts; something for which they were grateful, as they promptly ate him! From horses, his attention turned to women, warrior women to be exact. Now he had to get the belt of Hippolyta, Queen of the Amazons.

At first everything went well, with a warm welcome from the women to Hercules and his men, but the goddess Hera poisoned the minds of the Amazons against the men, and they had to fight for the belt and their lives. For task ten, Hercules had to find Geryon, the three-headed ogre and bring the king his cows. This involved travelling to an island off Africa, fighting Geryon's two-headed dog and killing the ogre. The eleventh task saw Hercules travel to the end of the earth, where Atlas held up the sky, to find the tree of Hesperides and from that tree pick three golden apples. Amazingly, the first eleven tasks took Hercules ten years. Imagine, ten years of his life, not to mention the fights, scraps and exhaustion involved, in search of the miracle of forgiveness from the gods.

But there's more, for he had yet to complete the twelfth and final task. For this he had to capture and return to the king, Cerberus, the dog that guards the underworld. This was no ordinary dog, for it had three heads, each head with a mane of writhing, hissing snakes. Charon, the old ferryman, took him across the river Styx into the underworld, where after a struggle, Hercules prevailed and returned the hideous creature to King Eurystheus, who it must be said, could have been a little more grateful. From the presence of the king, Hercules ran to the temple and heard the wonderful words he had waited years to hear: "The gods have forgiven you for killing your sons."[2]

Phew! I don't know about you, but I'm exhausted just thinking about the things Hercules had to do to receive the forgiveness he craved. Although none of us would ever want to go to such extremes to receive forgiveness, I believe there is something within the concept of working for our forgiveness which is attractive to us all. Doing something in order to get something makes us feel better. It justifies our position and gives us a sense of relief that we have contributed to the process of mercy and grace. Most religions and many cults carry this philosophy, where adherents must work, pray, fast, give or sacrifice in order to have the full acceptance of the deity they worship and attain the full enlightenment of the truth they covet.

2. *The Amazing Adventures of Hercules*, Usborne Paperbacks, UK, 2003. His Greek name is Heracles. Hercules is the Roman version and much better known.

However, the Bible teaches an amazing concept: that forgiveness is given freely and lavishly. The only catch: *we have to ask for it.*

Read slowly these amazing words:

*"But because of His great love for us, God who is rich in mercy, made us alive with Christ even when we were dead in transgressions..."*

It is by grace you have been saved...

*"For it is by grace you have been saved, through faith – and this not from yourselves, it is the gift of God – not by works, so that no-one can boast."* (Ephesians 2:4-5, 8-9)

It is interesting that the central part of the word "forgiven" is *give!* From the immensity of His love for us there flows a rich and wondrous river of grace, mercy and forgiveness to us. Initiated by His heart of love, its healing life has the power to transform every person who dares believe in such grace and throws themselves by faith into the river of mercy. Many hesitate because they are convinced, like Hercules, that forgiveness cannot be that easy; grace could not be given so liberally, and mercy must be earned. The love of God cries out to all who, with uncertainty, stand at the riverbank, bound by fear and ignorance. He calls to them, "Jump in! Bathe in grace, drink of love and be invigorated by the knowledge of total forgiveness, freely given."

I was born and raised in Northern Ireland. Its beauty is breathtaking and its people are among the friendliest in the world. Yet, in my growing-up years, during a period of history known hauntingly as "The Troubles", mind-numbing atrocities were committed in the name of religion and freedom. Thousands were killed and maimed throughout those years and they have become a shameful and bloody catalogue of our intolerance to those who are just a little different from us. I lost friends and family to the violence of those dark years and if not for the grace of God and the incredible love of my parents, I may have been lost too! In November 1987 a crowd of people were observing the Remembrance Day procession for those who had paid the ultimate price in the wars of the 20th Century. As they watched, a bomb exploded, killing eleven people and injuring sixty-three others. Under the mangled rubble, Marie Wilson, a twenty-three year old nurse reached out to her father and with her dying breath said, "Daddy, I love you very much." Gordon Wilson, her father, was left, like so many, with the pain of grief and the futile waste of a life so full of promise. However, Gordon was to shock the world with three little words. In a television interview, still bearing the scars of the dreadful events which had snatched away his beloved Marie, he said, "I forgive them."

The response to these words was incredible. People from all over Ireland and the world wrote to him and drew strength and inspiration from his simple yet dignified response. He had become a symbol of hope to millions and an inspiration to those experiencing the pain of vengeance and the emptiness of unforgiveness. For a moment, the world heard the heart of heaven in the words of this gentle Christian man. Gordon was not asked to forgive, but he did. Gordon didn't have to forgive, but he did. Gordon had an excuse not to forgive, but he forgave anyway.[3] In forgiving those who had so grievously wounded him, he allowed the light of heaven to touch a desperately dark world. Many reached for the light they saw in this tearful man, hopeful that they too could experience such grace.

The Bible declares of God that it is He, "... *Who forgives all your sins*." In Psalm 103 we have a proclamation of God's awesome love and an insight into mercy, which at times, beggars belief.

---

3. You can read about this remarkable journey and this outstanding man by reading the book simply entitled, *Marie*.

*"The Lord is compassionate and gracious, slow to anger, abounding in love. He will not always accuse, nor will he harbour his anger forever. He does not treat us as our sins deserve or repay us according to our iniquities. For as high as the heavens are above the earth, so great is His love for those who fear Him. As far as the east is from the west, so far has He removed our transgressions from us."* (Psalm 103:8-12)

Charles Spurgeon put it this way: "God soon turns from His wrath, but He never turns from His love." I am convinced, God is more willing to forgive than we are willing to accept the possibility of forgiveness.

When I was a child a wonderful new toy was released. It was called *Etch-a-Sketch*. I know it seems quaint in the light of our *.com* generation, but believe me, this was something to behold. This wondrous invention allowed me to draw to my heart's content and, once I'd finished, I could wipe the picture away with one movement of the handle. Literally, as I swiped it across the page, the image disappeared inch by inch until eventually the screen was blank. Cleared of what had been, I could now start all over again. It might have been cutting edge technology for a child, but the concept is not a new one. In fact, it's a biblical one!

*"I, even I, am He who blots out your transgressions, for my own sake, and remembers your sins no more."* (Isaiah 43:25)

Two amazing things happen when God forgives us:

Firstly, His mercy wipes away all the offence that has wounded Him and all that stops us from entering freely into His presence. It allows us to begin again, clean and unblemished. No shadow is left, no hidden reminder or undeleted files. *It has all gone!* If we are willing to confess our sins, He is willing to forgive. He blots out what was there and removes the stain of sin. Unfortunately, sometimes the consequences of sin remain with us. A murderer may seek forgiveness and find it, but he still has to serve his sentence. Yet, amazingly, if in sincerity and faith anyone asks for forgiveness, God gives it willingly, and that which corrupts is gone, forever!

Secondly, God chooses not to remember our sins. I have a fairly good memory, but I still forget stuff – sometimes because I'm trying to remember too much, or through lack of discipline, or because it never really registered in the first place. But God doesn't suffer from any of the weaknesses of human nature. He is perfect in every way. He cannot forget – unless of course He chooses to. In truth, it's not that God forgets, rather *He chooses not to remember*. I might remember how I offended my brother or hurt my wife or lusted after that woman, but if I have truly confessed and given it to God, He has already forgotten. Many times we remind God of things that He has decided not to remember and would prefer we did not remind Him of.

When Jesus came to earth He wanted to teach men and women about the heart of God. He was, after all, the exact representation of the Father, and if people were able to see and hear Him, then they would encounter the Divine, the One true and living God. Jesus often spoke to people looking for mercy and grace, who were burdened under man's interpretation of religious law, which left them destitute and bound to lifeless rules. "Keep the rules and you'll be okay," was the maxim of the day. However, tragically for many, they were keeping the rules but missing the point, for God's original rules were designed to point people to love not keep them from it.

How do you teach forgiveness to those who have forgotten what it looks like?

The greatest teaching tool on any subject is demonstration. Word sermons are good, but life sermons are by far the best way, and this is exactly what Jesus did. He chose to demonstrate love through forgiveness in some of the most controversial settings of His day, because through controversy, He could make His point and get the attention of the masses.

**Mad dogs and Samaritan women, go out in the noon day sun**
He watched her as she approached the well that day. Nothing unusual about that – after all, water was a precious commodity. What was different about this woman was that she came to the well during the hottest part of the day. Everyone else was under cover, but she came alone. This was a clear sign something was wrong, but Jesus did not judge her, He simply asked her for a drink. In this simple request Jesus crossed a million boundaries. He was a Jew, she a Samaritan. He was a man, she a woman. He was a rabbi, a teacher, a holy man, and she was a sinner. These rules were there for a reason, but Jesus ignored them, reaching out to her heart. We discover she had been through five marriages and was now living with a guy. Little wonder she had no friends and that she had to struggle getting the water up from the well on her own. As the conversation developed, Jesus talked more about living water that He had to offer than about her sin, which stood in the way. She knew she was a sinner. What she didn't know was that she could be forgiven! Incredibly, He told her "everything she ever did," but instead of feeling condemned she was invigorated to go and tell the town about what had happened, introducing them to the man who just might be the Messiah they had all been waiting for.

Because of her words, many came to see and believed in Him. But why would this woman want to introduce the town to a man who could dish *all* the dirt on her? The truth is, even though Jesus knew the truth, He chose to love and forgive. He did not use the knowledge of her sins to condemn her, but to liberate her. For the first time, for as long as she could remember, the burden of shame and guilt was gone and she enjoyed the liberty of grace, mercy and forgiveness.

What a lesson He taught that day. It blew the minds of His young Jewish apprentices, whose general opinion of Samaritans hovered somewhere between the status of pigs or dogs. It impacted the inhabitants of the town too, for of all the people the Messiah could have reached out to, this woman was surely bottom of the list. Yet He started with her and they willingly followed.

*"... Now we have heard for ourselves and we know that this man really is the Saviour of the world."*[4]

As one man put it:

"Love seeks only one thing: the good of the one loved."[5]

### Caught in the act

Had Jesus been a lawyer, the sensible thing would have been to pass this case to someone else. This was a done deal, a no-win situation. Caught red-handed and no doubt red-faced, she was guilty and according to the Law, she must die. It was just after dawn and the sun had barely warmed the earth when the woman was presented to Jesus. Her accusers were keen for her blood and for His. (By the way, any sign of the man she was with?)

*Can you see her?* Standing before the crowd, head down, clothes torn and face bloodied from the occasional righteous slap.

Ironically, she stood in the Temple courts, a place of prayer,

---

4. John 4:4-42.
5. Thomas Merton.

mercy and justice, but this was to be the place she would be judged and sentenced to death.

There was no point in protesting; after all she was just a woman and a filthy one at that. *Can you see her* – resigned to her fate? Before the day was out, her body would lie crushed beneath a ton of stones. In a few moments she would be handed over to the merciless crowd who would gladly extinguish her life. *Can you see her* – tears dripping silently from a once beautiful face? Perhaps she had been her father's princess. Perhaps she was someone's sister, daughter, wife or mother. Perhaps once, she had known love; somewhere far away she may have had a life. But now, she stands alone, about to die an unimaginably horrible death. She was guilty!

Asked His opinion on what should happen to her, Jesus said nothing at first. Instead, He stooped down and wrote something on the ground. I've got a few questions I want to ask Jesus when I get to heaven and this will be in my top three, *"What did you write on the ground that day?"* At first it didn't register, but standing up He invited the crowd to stone the woman. The only catch was, they had to be sinless to get the first throw. Then He went back to writing in the dirt. Was He writing the Law? Was it their sins? Was it the name of the man who had committed adultery with her and set her up? Whatever it was, the combination of that and His issued challenge slowly began to thin the crowd, until eventually only Jesus was left. Everyone, including those Jesus had been teaching that morning, uninvolved in this crime, had gone. Alone with Jesus the woman experienced love and forgiveness. She heard words of tenderness and life.

"... *neither do I condemn you, go now and leave your life of sin.*"[6]

*Can you see her?* She's now leaving the Temple forgiven and free, with a second chance to get life right and start all over again. She's still crying, but these are tears of joy and hope, for instead of dying today, she encountered life for the very first time. Determined, she leaves her life of sin and walks from that moment on in the power of forgiveness.

What a lesson Jesus taught that day and one everyone present would never forget. He did not contradict the Law or turn a blind eye to sin. Instead, in an awesome demonstration of grace, He managed to execute the Law in righteousness and turn a woman from a life of sin. In the Temple where so much blood was shed in search of forgiveness, the crowd and the nameless woman encountered divine forgiveness first hand.

By the way, as the woman left, I believe (and I can't prove it from the text) Jesus did one more thing. I believe He stooped down one more time and rubbed out whatever He had written on the ground. Only He, the crowd and the woman would ever know what was written, because even her accusers needed forgiveness.

## An unwelcome guest

Simon was a prominent Pharisee and he decided to throw a party and invite Jesus. Normally, on entering the house of a friend in those days, a guest could expect some water to wash their feet, or in certain circumstances, someone to do it for them. The host would extend the kiss of friendship as he welcomed his guests and it was not a bad thing to offer some perfumed oil to mask the many body odours which may be floating around due to the heat of the day.

---

6. John 8:1-11.

None of these graces were offered to Jesus when He entered Simon's home, and to those present, they understood how insulting this was to any guest, but Jesus said nothing.

During the all-male party, a woman decided to gate crash. She was not just any woman, for the Bible says she "… lived a sinful life in the town…" Yet, on entering Simon's house, she went straight to Jesus and started to do to Him the things Simon should have done, and more. Standing behind Him, she wet His unwashed feet with her tears and wiped them clean with her hair. Then she kissed them and poured perfume on them. Her perfume filled the air and no-one could escape its fragrance. I love how John Ortberg puts it: "She has been so broken and undone by his sheer goodness that it is as if she has forgotten who she is and where she is, and she unashamedly pours herself out in adoration and gratitude."[7]

Jesus knew who she was, what she had done, where she had come from and why she was doing what she was doing, but He did not stop her, nor was He afraid to let her touch Him. We should learn a lesson from this – that God is not afraid of sinners getting too close to Him. He's much more willing for them to get closer than self-righteous religious types could ever cope with. He loves sinners and doesn't have a problem with them at all.

To conclude the lesson that day, Jesus told a simple story. Two men owed money to a moneylender. One owed a huge amount; the other, by comparison, just a little. Neither of them could pay back what they had borrowed, so the money-lender cancelled the debts of both men. Jesus asked the question, "Now which one of them will love him more?" Simon replied, "I suppose the one who had the bigger debt cancelled."

The conclusion was profoundly powerful.

If a person is aware of how much they have been forgiven and how great the debt they owed, then in turn, their love for the one who cancelled the debt will be great. Simon was as much a sinner as this woman in the estimation of heaven, but he didn't know it and certainly didn't think it.

That's why he treated Jesus so glibly when He entered his home. On the other hand, the sinful woman was very aware of how great her debt was and the power of cancellation. As a result she lavished her love on Jesus without reservation or embarrassment. Note Jesus' conclusion on the matter when speaking to the woman: "Your sins are forgiven."

What a lesson Jesus taught that evening. Sinners can get close and sinners can be forgiven. Sinners can be changed from rebels to lovers, all as a result of love and grace. Simon and his friends saw first hand the power of forgiveness at work, but also how easy it can be to miss it when it is viewed from a judgemental and self-righteous perspective. The woman had been offered the opportunity to have her enormous debt cancelled and she took it with both hands.

Hercules spent ten years of his life searching for forgiveness, earning the right to have it. For you and I it is much simpler. As unbelievable as it sounds, God's love is such that we only have to ask for it, presenting our sinfulness to Him and He will do the rest. A true understanding of God's forgiveness takes the emphasis away from us and onto Him. He initiates the process of forgiveness and completes it by blotting our sins out and making the choice never to remember them again. This is none of our doing, rather it is all of His doing. God's forgiveness cannot be earned, it can only be accepted. He is ready and willing to forgive. We only need ask!

*"If we confess our sins, He is faithful and just and will forgive us our sins and purify us from all unrighteousness."* (1 John 1:9)

# Chapter 6
## Licensed to Sin?

"Love so amazing so divine, demands my soul, my life, my all."[1]

Grigori Yefimovich Novykh has been described as one of the most scandalous figures in Russian history. In 1903 he arrived in St. Petersburg, then capital of Russia, from his home in Pokrovskoe, Siberia in the robes of a monk, as a self-styled holy man or "staretz". Though a semi-literate peasant, within a few years he became one of the most influential men in the Russian government. The world knows him as Rasputin. This was a nickname, given to him, meaning "dissolute" or "debauched" in Russian. With a reputation as a drunkard and womaniser, he certainly lived up to his name. In late 1908, General Dedylin, responsible for the Tsar's security, presented a report to Nicholas II documenting Rasputin's unsavoury actions, including outings to bathhouses, beatings and violent sex with society women and prostitutes. He rarely washed or changed his clothes, leaving his appearance ragged and his hair greasy. However this, along with his intense personal magnetism and his piercing blue eyes, only served to convince his followers that he was indeed a "man of God".[2]

1. Isaac Watts, *When I Survey the Wondrous Cross.*
2. www.worsleyschool.net and www.channel4.com (Masters of Darkness series).

The pop-group Boney M sang about the "mad monk" bringing his name to a modern audience. If you haven't heard the song, I'm not sure you've missed much, and if you have heard it, I apologise for this reminder, but why should I suffer alone? The lyrics are an interesting take on history, containing such literary gems as, *"Most people looked at him with terror and with fear, but to Moscow chicks he was such a lovely dear"*![3]

I'll give you a moment to appreciate this cultural experience. Okay, that's enough! Rasputin is a paradoxical character. A self-styled "man of God" with a track record of supernatural occurrences, yet he lived a lifestyle of such extreme moral recklessness that even the most liberal thinking person would be shocked. How could he do this?

Rasputin had developed his own theology from various cults and sects, believing that a person had to sin in order to become holy. He taught and exemplified the doctrine that salvation could be attained by repeated acts of sin and repentance. He reasoned that those who sin require the most forgiveness, therefore a sinner who continues to sin, experiences more of God's grace than any ordinary sinner. Rasputin taught that when it comes to sin, righteousness and our relationship with God, it is possible to have your cake and eat it!

This was not a new idea, so be careful not to credit it to the Siberian Monk. This "theology" is as old as the Bible. The Apostle Paul wrote to the Roman church on the great doctrine of justification by faith, expounding the many facets of the grace, mercy and love of God.

The book of Romans is a masterpiece of theological development and reasoning, leaving no stone unturned. In the middle of the book Paul asks a question:

3. www.lyricsDepot.com

*"So what do we do? Keep on sinning so God can keep on forgiving? I should hope not!"* (Romans 6:1)[4]

On hearing the immense teaching on the love and grace of God, some concluded that Paul was advocating, "Let us do evil that good may result."[5] But this was the furthest thing from his mind, conclusively refuting the idea by answering his own question.

*"By no means! We died to sin; how can we live in it any longer?"* (Romans 6:2.)

Antinomianism sounds like something you would expect to find in a tropical diseases research clinic, but in fact it is a word which describes the theological conflict Paul was fighting and the lifestyle Rasputin gave himself to. The word literally means "against the law" and it was a term given to those who held that the moral law is not binding upon believers as a rule of life, and that a believer can sin with impunity because the grace of God super-abounds over their sin.[6]

For a number of years now I have been passionately teaching that God loves us and that the knowledge of being loved can transform the way we live. As I have written so far in this book, with God's love there are no strings attached and no small print; that through His love He accepts us, forgives us and, if we submit to Him, transforms us. When I teach this, someone often raises the concern that this sort of teaching will encourage people to take advantage of the love of God, live how they want and still expect grace and forgiveness. The argument runs, "If people get the idea that God loves them, no matter what, and that God will forgive them, no matter how they live, it will liberate them to sin, knowing the grace of God will bail them out." They listen to the message

---

4. Peterson, E.H., *The Message*, 1993.
5. Romans 3:8.
6. Cairns, A., *Dictionary of Theological Terms*, 1982, p.5.

of the love of God and see only the danger of a liberal lifestyle that probes for the loophole, instead of rejoicing in the freedom of empowered responsibility. Many give intellectual assent to the love of God, but deep down worry about the implications of the freedom it brings and the fact that people may take advantage of it. So, legislation is established to combat liberalism. Rules are enshrined, just in case people decide to go too far, and penalties are in place to punish those who presume too much.

Please don't get me wrong, we need rules and guidelines in order for life to operate. But when it comes to the love of God, I suspect we legislate to protect our own hang-ups, insecurities and anxieties about how we think people should behave, rather than protecting the great doctrine of the love of God from abuse. God's love does not need protecting and, whether we like it or not, regardless of the absence or presence of rules, humanity has been "taking advantage" of heaven's love for as long as we have been on the earth. Legalism can't combat liberalism, only love can. For centuries the Church has tried to get people to do the right things as a reflection of their commitment to God and truth. The rules kept people in line, but did not change them. People will only fulfil the law, and keep the law, if the law is written on their hearts. That only happens when they truly engage with and understand the love of God. Without this knowledge of His love, whether they have rules or not, they will ultimately do what they want and not what He wants.

### Keeping the rules but missing the point

"Are you saying we shouldn't have any rules to stop people sinning and taking advantage of God's love? Should we just let them do what they want?" some may protest. No, of course I'm not saying that, but the Bible and experience has taught me that rules alone are not a deterrent in stopping people from sinning or even getting them to do the right thing. Furthermore, even if we keep all the rules but keep them for the wrong reason, though this is good, by God's reckoning, it is not the best.

Imagine the scene. I'm sitting with my wife in a top class restaurant. Candles illuminate the table as we look at each other, celebrating our 50th wedding anniversary. I push a little box containing something sparkly at her and she smiles and acts surprised as if she wasn't expecting anything. As we eat, the violinist is playing romantically just for us. Then I tell her the secret of my faithfulness. "Darling, we've been together as man and wife for 50 years. In that time you are the only woman I've ever been with. You have been the only woman for me." Smiling seductively she asks, "Why?" and tenderly I explain, "Because the Bible says not to commit adultery!"

The violinist has gone, someone has blown the candles out and my sparkly, expensive gift now lies in the bin. "Was it something I said?" I did the right thing, but for the wrong reason. Who reading this knows it was the wrong answer?! My motivation for being faithful should be because *I love my wife*, not because a rule says I can't have another woman. The rule is good, but the point is love!

"I've never cheated on my wife" – *but do you love her?*

"I tithe" – *but are you generous?*

"I don't criticise" – *but do you encourage?*

"I read my Bible" – *but do you live it?*

"I like the modern songs" – *but do you worship?*

"I love coming to Church" – *but do you love the people?*

On the surface, rule keeping can suggest we've got the point, but if we're not careful, rule keeping distracts us from the point.

As a parent I see this every day. In the instruction of our children, as delightful as our little angels are, there is a continual struggle for the heart. Often my children do things simply because they've been asked (or threatened... I know you've never done this). They comply without changing. They obey without understanding. They've kept the rule, tidied their room, brushed their teeth, stopped arguing, but they've missed the point of why they have been asked to do this in the first place. When the reason becomes an issue of the heart, they will do what they must and keep the rules without being asked. Will that happen soon?

To stop people taking advantage of God's love, religion has gone to extraordinary lengths. By the time Jesus turned up, the *Ten Commandments* had been, how shall we put it, "expanded" slightly. The mentality was "make a fence for the law", carry the prohibitions beyond the written law to protect them from the temptation to sin. So when Jesus was asked what the greatest commandment was, it was a loaded question. Whatever He said was bound to offend and cause an eruption of theological debate and division of mind-numbing proportions. So what did He say was the greatest commandment?

*"Hear O Israel, the Lord our God the Lord is One. Love the Lord your God with all your heart and with all your soul and with all your mind and with all your strength. The second is this: love your neighbour as yourself."* (Mark 12:30-31)

Those experts listening to Him had spent most of their lives developing the Law, learning every letter and meaning, debating endlessly about the implications of disobedience. But for all their zeal and dedication, they had strained gnats and swallowed camels in the estimation of the Master. Although they had kept the rules, they had missed the point and encouraged those who followed them to miss it also. In one incredible moment, Jesus summed up the Law and the Prophets in two short sentences. He wiped away the pretentiousness of self-righteousness and the need to protect the Law or God's love from abuse. Jesus taught His audience that day that the point is love – and if we don't keep the rules out of love, then the rules themselves have no real point. Jesus came to demonstrate the love of God to a dying world. His mission was that hearts would truly engage with God's love and, in return, love God back; a love expressed not in the license of sin, but in simple obedience to truth.

*"If you love Me, you will obey what I command."* (John 14:15)

The point of the rule is not to keep us from sin, but rather direct us to love. I will do the right thing for the right reasons when love lives within in; when the central focus in my life is loving God and living in His love, having received it from Him in the first place. Love, not the rules, prevents me from taking advantage of this glorious love, for when no-one is around to check up on me, to make sure I'm living right, love ensures I do!

Are you missing the point? Have you sought to diligently keep the rules without really knowing why? Are you endeavouring to do what is right without the power of love to assist you?

The battle against sin is hard enough. We must not seek to win this fight without the knowledge that we are loved and that our love for God is at the heart of all we are and everything we do.

When we are loved by God and we passionately love Him in return, we will do what He wants.

**Do the sums**
Paul said,

*"In the same way, count yourselves dead to sin but alive to God in Christ Jesus."* (Romans 6:11)

The word translated "count" is interesting. Properly used it is a term of numerical calculation, and by using it the way he does, Paul is encouraging us to do the sums, leave nothing to chance or guess work; know the truth and get the facts.

All our children have had pocket money boxes. Every so often they were allowed to dip into them for various things, or to buy *me* ice-cream. Before opening their box to give them some money, I sometimes ask, "How much do you think you have?" How optimistic they felt at that moment would dictate the estimate. They didn't know exactly, but they had a guess. There have been times when they were delighted with the knowledge that there was more than they thought, as well as disappointed when they learnt their financial reserves were well below what they hoped. The only way to truly know is to do the sums and keep a record.

Paul understands that this is a vital key to living in the freedom of God's love and overcoming the temptation of license to sin. Simply telling the Roman believers not to do it will not work; he must give them a reason, power and truth. When it comes to living in the power of God's love and fighting sin, guess work is not good enough; it just won't cut it. If we're going to live as God intended, we've got to *know*, and the only way we can know is to sit down and do the sums. We need to get the Word and our calculator out and start adding things up. As we do we'll be amazed at what God has done, who we are and what we've got. Love and knowledge are a powerful combination.

Doing the sums moves us from the realm of our feelings, fantasy and fiction and into the land of facts. What we think or feel may not be true and it is our responsibility to move beyond the boundaries of such shallow reasoning and engage with what is fact. Ignorance keeps us in the dark and strips us of power. Without the knowledge of the truth we are at the mercy of whatever comes over the horizon of our lives. We are powerless to resist any whim of doctrine or feeling of insecurity or suggestion from the enemy. If we are going to live in the power of love and live above the license to sin, we must know the truth. You and I must sit down and reckon up what is true and what is not. Only then do we have a chance of living in freedom.

**Fact:** Through baptism you were buried with Christ (Romans 6:3)

**Fact:** Through His resurrection we can have new life (6:4)

**Fact:** Our old self has been crucified with Christ (6:6)

**Fact:** Through that death, we are no longer slaves to sin (6:7)

It is easy to look at such facts and judge them in the light of our experience, our feelings or our understanding. But this is where the challenge comes to apply what we've discovered by doing our sums – reckoning up that which we previously knew and allowed to govern our lives. Love brings us into new knowledge, but we must have the courage to apply this knowledge to our lives, thus leading us to freedom. Paul instructed them that the key to getting the facts was in obeying the teaching given to them.

*"…You wholeheartedly obeyed the form of teaching to which you were entrusted." (6:17)*

The Word contains the Truth. Don't leave your life to guess work. Do the sums and know the facts. Knowing moves us to a position of choice. Paul is clear that when it comes to living free or living in sin: those who are in the love of Christ have a choice.

*"… do not let sin reign in your mortal body." (6:12)*

*"Do not offer the parts of your body to sin…" (6:13)*

*"For sin shall not be your master…" (6:14)*

All of these are choices. We have the power to offer or not, to give ourselves to sin or righteousness, to please God or please ourselves. Having come to Christ, the choice is now ours. It is not inevitable that we will sin. We do not live at the mercy of sin. Rather, love empowers us with the ability to choose. That's why our choices must be made from the right premise. If we choose because of our fear of the rules, we'll fail. If we choose because of what we feel or think might be right, we'll fail. Our choices must flow from a heart empowered by the love of God and the knowledge of His truth. When these two principles are flowing together in our lives by faith, we have the power to choose what is right and the ability to live what we choose.

**The Samson syndrome**
The longhaired lover from Mahaneh Dan had an incredible beginning. Born from a sterile womb, his life was full of promise and he was destined to be a deliverer in the purposes of God. This he eventually did, although the Bible adds an epitaph, *"Thus he killed many more when he died than when he lived"* (Judges 16:30). Samson liked the girls and they clearly liked him, but they weren't the problem, only the symptom. The great sin of Samson's life was presumption. When lying in the lap of Delilah he played a dangerous game and lost. Little by little she got closer to the truth, until eventually the secret of his strength was out. As he awoke to reality he thought,

*"I'll go out as before and shake myself free."* (Judges 16:20)

However, the tragic fact was this:

*"But he did not know that the Lord had left him."* (verse 20)

God did not leave Samson because He suddenly stopped loving his reckless servant. He left him because Samson presumed He would always be there, no matter what. Throughout his life, Samson had read the signals wrong, misunderstanding the grace of God and crossing the line into abusing the love of God. Yet, God continued to love, forgive and empower, while Samson continued to miss the point. We rarely see the young man praying. In fact he only prays twice (15:18 and 16:28). He lived for self-satisfaction and only at the end of his life did he consider the will of God over his own.

Samson made two crucial mistakes, which affirmed him in his presumption and strengthened him in his license to sin.

**He mistook the mercy of God for the blessing of God.**

It is arguable that every time the Spirit of God came on Samson it was in some capacity to get him out of trouble. Check out 14:6, 9 and 15:14. I can remember being in Sunday School hearing the great story of Samson carrying the city gates on his shoulders. But then I read the story and discovered the man of God had been with a prostitute the night before. However, every time Samson got away with it. Somehow God kept showing up, kept getting him out of trouble and kept granting him deliverance. Samson mistook God's mercy for His blessing. "I did it before, I can do it again ... God helped me last time, He will help me this time ... God loves me, He's for me ... He won't abandon me." Time after time, God kept lavishing His love on His boy, but the boy just wasn't getting it.

**He misunderstood the forgiveness of God for the sanction of God.**

In chapter fourteen of Judges, Samson is after a woman. Nothing

LOVED

wrong with that, except she was the type of woman God had forbidden him to have. Even his father tried to talk him out of it, but to no avail. "Get her for me. She's the right one for me" (verse 3). Not only did he get her (although the relationship was short lived), but then he got another and another. In the record of Samson's life, all the women involved are Philistine women. He had not learned from his first experience. She was a Philistine but Samson still had his strength; the Spirit of God was still coming on him and God was still blessing him. "It must be okay to do what I am doing," he thought. He confused the fact that God's forgiveness of his sin did not mean He sanctioned his lifestyle – in fact, it was the opposite. Somehow, Samson got the signals wrong and presumed on God's love and mercy. That presumption was to cost him dear. In my opinion Samson died too soon, he died the wrong way, and he died not having fulfilled his true potential in God. However, he died loved!

The story, of course, doesn't end in failure, but victory and Samson, by God's grace, is listed in the great Hall of Faith of Hebrews chapter 11. But we must not lose sight of that which the life of this young man teaches us. God is love and He never stops loving us, but as Samson teaches us, if we presume that His lavish love is the license for a lifestyle of sin, then at some point we will start paying the price for the decisions made. Samson lived the life he did because he did not understand the heart and nature of God, nor it seems did he have the slightest clue as to what he had and what it was for. In the light of such ignorance, not having done the sums or understood the *law of love*, which lies at the heart of a relationship with God, it is not surprising that Samson lived to please himself.

For centuries people have grappled with the issues associated with love and license. It is a difficult challenge, but one made easier when we understand something of the love about which we are talking and the God who is love. As we see God's love for what it truly is, we are drawn to its beauty and captivated by its magnificence. The more we grasp this love, the less we want to live for ourselves and the more we want to live for Him. I believe in the liberalism which the love of God brings, but not the liberalism of living for self; rather the liberty to live fully and unreservedly for Him.

One of my favourite hymns of all time was written by a man called Isaac Watts. The words are simple yet profound and they capture the essence of the truth I have sought to teach in this chapter. If we see His love, know His love and live in His love, having a license to sin will be the last thing on our mind. I leave you to ponder his inspiring words:

*When I survey the wondrous cross,*
*on which the Prince of glory died,*
*My richest gain I count but loss,*
*and pour contempt on all my pride.*
*Forbid it, Lord, that I should boast,*
*save in the death of Christ my God:*
*All the vain things that charm me most,*
*I sacrifice them to His blood.*
*See from His head, His hands, His feet,*
*sorrow and love flow mingled down;*
*Did e'er such love and sorrow meet,*
*or thorns compose so rich a crown?*
*Were the whole realm of nature mine,*

*that were an offering far too small;*

*Love so amazing, so divine,*

*demands my soul, my life, my all.*[7]

Remember, the freedom of love is not the license to sin.

---

7. *The New Redemption Hymnal*, no.227.

# Chapter 7
## Live Like You Belong

"He (God) has a curious fantasy of making all these disgusting little human vermin into what He calls His 'free' lovers and servants – 'sons' is the word He uses..."[1]

The alarm clock had buzzed, Dawn was already in the shower, Elaina my eldest daughter was in the other bathroom getting washed and ready for school and Beth-Anne, the baby of the bunch, was standing at the top of the stairs singing her lungs out. I had been granted a few minutes of slumber as I waited for my call to the running shower. As I snoozed, thinking that it couldn't be that time already, my bed moved. My son Simeon was quietly but purposefully burrowing himself under the covers and making his way towards me. I pretended not to notice his approach, but soon he was beside me. He snuggled up, put his arms gently over my chest, kissed me, and in a baby voice said, "Da Da." As I opened my eyes and looked at him, he was smiling an exaggerated sort of smile, which highjacked his whole face, then he said these words, "I love you Da da!" For a few moments, I was lost in wonder. The pressures, deadlines and demands of the coming day were forgotten.

---

1. Lewis, *The Screwtape Letters*, p.17. My brackets insertion.

I wasn't Pastor John, Dr John, the fount of all knowledge, or God's man of power for the hour, I was "Da da" and I was loved.

We love snuggles and hugs in our house. We're a tactile home, so touching, hugging, kissing, snuggling and even pinching bottoms are all part of our routine. Mind you, it did get me into trouble once. My son saw how I would regularly pinch Dawn (my wife's) bottom, so he decided that's how boys behaved... in church! We had a father son chat on why church bums are out of bounds when it comes to pinching. In our home these things are not only signs of affection, they are demonstrations of belonging. Elaina, Simeon and Beth-Anne can get snuggles any time, because they belong. It's their right, their privilege and their joy. My son climbed into my bed and snuggled, because he knew he was loved, he knew he was accepted and he knew he belonged.

The Bible declares that God is love. We've seen this amazing truth already. But the Bible goes even further in calling God our Father. For those who reach out to Him by faith, there is the prospect of entering into a dynamic, intimate, personal relationship with the God who is love, thus understanding and experiencing His incredible love first hand.

*"Yet to all who received Him, to those who believed in His name, He gave the right to become children of God."* (John 1:12)

It is one thing to be given the right to be called a child of God; it is another thing entirely to live like a child of God. Many know this truth in their theology, but fail to live in the reality of it day by day. They know God is a Father, but would not even dream of *snuggling*. This knowledge has yet to make the greatest journey of all, from the head to the heart. It's only a few inches, but it can be a long, long way. God, your Father, wants you to live like you belong. Sonship (and when I use that term it is generic including both male and female) as God intended it, is more than a guarantee to heaven, though that is wonderful. Rather, it is the Father's ambition that we experience fullness of life and love with Him and out of that intimate knowledge of our *lovedness*, grow strong, give more and live well. Truly understanding our sonship is not merely a passport to life after death, but the guarantee of living before death.

**How can we live like we belong?**

For me, the best example of a son living well and living like he belonged to the Father is Jesus Himself. We sometimes forget that although He was God and the Saviour of the world, He was also a son! As I've meditated on the life of Jesus, I have been drawn to some words the Father spoke to Him before His ministry actually began. I believe that these words contain some powerful revelation keys to help us live as if we belong. They did for Jesus, and they can for us.

John is baptising people in the Jordan as Jesus approaches. They have a brief conversation in which John tries to deter Jesus from doing what He is about to do, but to no avail. Jesus is baptised by John in the river, along with many other people. As He's coming out of the water, the Bible says that in an act of definite intention, "*... heaven was opened...*" (Mark's Gospel says it was *torn open*), the Holy Spirit descended like a dove and a voice spoke:

"*This is my Son, whom I love; with Him I am well pleased.*" (Matthew 3:17)

In these words, I believe there are four crucial keys to help any child of God live like they belong. As a Son, Jesus knew and lived them, and out of these truths, He impacted the world.

**We will live like we belong when we know the Father**

The assumption is made that the Father spoke to Jesus that day and it is a safe one to make. After all, He refers to Jesus as His Son. However, what is interesting is that the Bible, in the accounts found in Matthew, Mark and Luke, does not say it was the Father speaking, but rather described the speaker in terms of "a voice".

*Everyone heard a voice that day, but Jesus heard the Father!*

As I write, there are approximately one and a half million people living in Northern Ireland, and of those born and raised there, they will all have Ulster accents. Yet, if my father came on the phone and spoke to me, I would know it was him! I know him, have an intimate relationship with him and can tell the difference between his voice and that of any other Irish person. Jesus picked up on this when He said of the Good Shepherd that,

"... *His sheep follow Him because they know His voice.*"

(John 10:4)

The sheep would not be expected to follow a stranger, they would only follow someone they knew.

That day in the Jordan, Jesus knew the voice was the Father. He had heard that voice many times before. He knew the heart and nature of the Father, and over many years as a man had come to trust and obey that voice. Some may have heard *a voice*, others that day heard *a noise*, or what sounded like thunder. They may have been confused because they did not know the Father, but Jesus heard clearly, because He knew *His voice*.

We will never live like we belong, if we do not come to know the Father who gave us life in the first place. If our Father remains a distant, mysterious figure, to be approached only when invited, we will struggle to truly take our place as a son or daughter in His House and in His presence. Over the years, I have listened to those who have been deeply wounded by their biological fathers express the view that because of their pain they will never be able to look on God as their Father. For them this image is forever tainted. As a young minister I used to accept this conclusion and shrug my shoulders in agreement. Now, I challenge it. Everything we know about God the Father comes to us by faith and revelation of the truth. Our understanding of Him is not dependent on any human relational experience we may have had, whether good or bad. I was raised in a wonderful home, with great parents and with love in abundance. You may have been raised in the closest thing to hell this side of the grave, but the incredible fact is, *we both need revelation of the Father if we are to approach Him, know Him and love Him.* The fact that one dad was good and the other bad has no bearing on how we see God the Father. It is the same for us all. So, to flip the coin for a moment, it is possible to be raised by a wonderful father and yet not know Father-God. It is possible to be raised by a brute who called himself a father, and yet today live in the freedom of knowing *Abba Father*! Revelation is the key to knowing Him and knowing Him is vital to living like we belong.

**We will live like we belong when we know who we are**
*"This is My Son…"*

Jesus knew He was the Son of the Father. Whatever His social status, He knew that He had a Father in heaven, but He also knew He was the Father's Son!

Now be honest with me, when you've been doing your daily Bible reading programme, and you came to the genealogies, those long lists of unpronounceable names, did you read them the whole way through or were you tempted to speed read and skip on to the good bits? For years when I came to those lists, I used to move over them quickly. I knew there must be some reason for them, but I just couldn't think what it could be.

Both Matthew and Luke include a historical name list for Jesus, although Matthew starts with Abraham and Luke goes all the way back to God. Take a moment to read the names; there are lots of them. Have you ever wondered why those names are there? I suspect it has something to do with discovering who we are. To truly know who we are, we have to know where we came from and what we're a part of. If Jesus looked back and saw that list of names, He would understand that life wasn't an accident, that He wasn't alone, and important as His life was, it was the product of many other factors. The list gives a sense of perspective, allowing us to grasp the bigger picture. The list gives an understanding of purpose, for in understanding where we've come from it helps us receive a clearer focus on where we need to go. But the list also gives us a sense of personhood. This is who I am, the son of... who was the son of... who was the son of...!

A number of years ago, someone came up with the idea of allowing prospective parents (single or married) the freedom to walk into a donor clinic, pay their money, select the sperm that was best for them and, from that, help produce a baby. As a result thousands of children, many of them now young adults, were born, most of them healthy, intelligent and genetically strong. Today many of those children are searching for connection. They want to know where they have come from and who they came from. Although the programme proved a success in terms of giving parents what they wanted, it has left many sons and daughters incomplete in their identity. Being alive is not enough for humanity, we need to know who we are and where we came from. That's the way we've been designed and that's what helps us make the connections to live like we belong.

### Do you know who you are?

*"How great is the love the Father has lavished on us, that we should be called children of God! **And that is what we are!**"* (1 John 3:1)

### We will live like we belong when we know we are loved

*"... Whom I love..."*

J. Wilbur Chapman often told of the testimony given in one of his meetings by a certain man:

"I got off at the Pennsylvania depot as a tramp, and for a year I begged on the streets for a living. One day I touched a man on the shoulder and said, 'Hey, mister, can you give me a dime?' As soon as I saw his face, I was shocked to see that it was my own father. I said, 'Father, father, do you know me?' Throwing his arms around me and with tears in his eyes, he said, 'Oh my son, at last I've found you! I've found you. You want a dime? Everything I have is yours.' Think of it. I was a tramp. I stood begging my own father for ten cents, when for eighteen years he had been looking for me to give me all that he had."[2]

The tragedy for many wonderful Christians is that they live as if unloved, when they are loved beyond words. They are hoping for "dimes" when wealth and riches await. They settle for scraps, when a banqueting table has been set for a feast; beg for shelter and warmth when His banner over them is love! To understand that we are loved is the single most important revelation key of our lives. Nothing in all the annals of Christian literature or theology

2. *Bible Illustrator*, Parsons, 1997.

is more important than this fact. Know this and everything else falls into place. If we get this, the world will open up to us, opportunity will smack us in the face, life will become enjoyable and serving King Jesus will be our number one priority. When we know we are loved, life gets a whole lot better. When we know the Father loves us, serving Him is not an issue or a challenge.

"Why weep? I do not know. Perhaps it is because of the utter gratuitousness of life, of being, which we experience in such moments, like the occasions when we know what it is to be loved, truly, deeply, for ourselves."[3]

## We will live like we belong when we understand we are valued for *who*, not *what*

One of Morrie Schwartz's first jobs was working in a mental institution called Chestnut Lodge. He had been given a grant to observe mental patients and record their treatments. He had many stories to tell of his five years at Chestnut Lodge and this is just one of them.

"One of the patients, a middle-aged woman, came out of her room every day and lay facedown on the tile floor, staying there for hours as doctors and nurses stepped around her. Morrie watched in horror. He took notes, which was what he was there to do. Every day she did the same thing: came out in the morning, lay on the floor, stayed there until the evening, talking to no one, ignored by everyone. It saddened Morrie. He began to sit on the floor with her, even lay down alongside her, trying to draw her out of her misery. Eventually, he got her to sit up and even to return to her room.

---

3. Ward, H., & Wild, J., *The Lion Christian Quotation Collection*, UK, 1997, p.243.

What she mostly wanted, he learned, was the same thing many people want: *someone to notice she was there.*"[4] With no contribution to make she was deemed of no real value. Imprisoned and abandoned, no one seemed to care at all, and every day she made her small but dramatic protest, until somebody took the time to notice. Had she been a rich lady sitting in an expensive car, with influence and position, no one would have passed her by. But the truth was that to many she was nobody, nothing. What was her name anyway?

Sometimes, if we are not careful, we become convinced that God only values us because of what we can do for Him, rather than *who* we are. I grew up in a Pentecostal church full of activity. Do you know the rhyme?

*Mary had a little lamb, was given her to keep.*

*It joined a Pentecostal church and died through lack of sleep.*

As a family we went to church four times on a Sunday and then there were all the mid-week activities on top. So I have always been comfortable with faith expressing itself in service, church attendance and programmes. However, a subtle temptation lurks in such busyness:

"The more I do, the more important I am and the more God will love me. He doesn't love me because of what I do, of course not, but I'm sure it helps, just a little."

The truth is we work out of love – *not for it!*

The Father told Jesus He was well pleased with Him before Jesus had done anything. Up to this moment He had not preached, preformed a miracle, walked on water or fed thousands of people with a packed lunch. He had lived a relatively quiet life in Galilee and for most of His thirty years on the planet He kept out of the spotlight.

---

4. Albom, op.cit., pp.109-110.

So what was God so pleased about?

Traditionally, I believed this statement was in response to Jesus being baptised, and I am still comfortable with that thought. But could it be that the Father was pleased with Him simply because He loved Him? Could it be the Father was expressing His pleasure in His Son, before His Son had even started His ministry? Could it be the Father was in love with the *who*, not just the *what*? If Jesus was pleasing the Father before He did anything, then maybe there is something the Father is more interested in than our doing.

Too many of us, and I have been there and got a whole range of T-shirts on this one, work for love, hoping to earn the pleasure of the Father. However, our motivation should not be *for* love, but *because of* love. Having come into the knowledge of God's love for our lives, we please Him! Jesus knew these four crucial truths and out of them, I believe He was able to minister more effectively. Yes, He received the power of the Holy Spirit that day, equipping Him to perform amazing things, but He also heard the affirming words of the Father, words of intimacy, love and pleasure. When we grasp such truth, the knowledge that we are loved, will empower us to live like we belong and prevent us from settling for *second-class sonship*.

**The mind of a slave in the body of a son.**

Jesus told the story of a father with two sons. One son wanted to leave home, but the other stayed. When the son who left came home, the father threw a party, which annoyed the son who had stayed. His words reveal his heart. Listen carefully:

*"Look! All these years I've been slaving for you and never disobeyed your orders..."* (Luke 15:29)[5]

---

5. My italics.

He was a son but he lived like a slave. Locked into a "duty culture", he never dared understand the father or embrace the wealth that was his: *"... everything I have is yours"* (verse 31). Instead, he did what a good son should without ever experiencing the freedom and life that a son of the house should enjoy. He was a son, but never grasped why! In my years of ministry I've met many of them: *sons with a slave mentality.* They work, do their duty, but never enjoy. Their value is locked up in their doing, not their being, and as a result they wait in the shadows for an invitation to party, when they can party any time.

**The heart of a squatter at the table of the king.**
David wanted to honour his promise to his best friend Jonathan. After Jonathan's death he opened his home to Jonathan's children. Mephibosheth, who was crippled in both feet was brought before the king, addressing himself to David as a "dead dog". David extended grace and generosity to the young man and the Bible says:

*"So Mephibosheth ate at David's table like one of the king's sons."*
(2 Samuel 9:11)

However, when David's life was in danger and he had to leave Jerusalem, Mephibosheth stayed behind, believing that his grandfather's throne (King Saul) would be returned to him. Though offered the position of a son, in mentality, it seems, he remained a squatter in the house of the king, eating from his table, but never understanding what was going on around him. The young man took his seat but struggled to take possession of the truth. Eventually reconciled to David, Mephibosheth hesitated to live like a son of the king because he felt as if he did not belong.

A squatter is someone who takes possession of a property or piece of land they do not truly own. They live there, but because they have never properly taken ownership, they exist with the threat of eviction. "Any time now, the police will come to evict me." "Any minute now, David will throw me to the dogs." The squatter knows the constant insecurity of life without ownership; of position without power. Too many wonderful Christians live like this. They sit at the table, looking around in wonder, but thinking that it is for someone else. They feel they don't belong because they've never taken ownership of the invitation to sit at his table "like one of his sons".

## The craving for satisfaction in the house of plenty

*"Father give me my share of the estate."* (Luke 15:12)

Why did the young son in Jesus' story leave?

"Come on, you know young men, restless for adventure. He just wanted to see the world and find his own way. He wanted to discover life beyond the boundaries of his home..."

Was it possible for the young man to have done all that, without spending his inheritance and leaving home? Did his actions have to be so extreme or could he have remained in relationship and still seen the world?

It is interesting that when he came to his senses, he started thinking of home, but he still didn't understand. That was the reason he left in the first place, because he never understood what he had. We say it sometimes, don't we, "You don't know what you've got until it's gone." But for this young man, though he headed for home, it was with the hope of becoming a hired servant, not being welcomed as a son! He still hadn't got it. He left as a son without ever knowing what being a son meant, therefore

LIVE LIKE YOU BELONG

when he blew his money and returned home, because he still didn't understand what a son was, he settled for being a servant.

Don't judge him too harshly, we do it all the time. Christians who have little understanding of who they are, search for more when they already have everything they need. We live in the realm of the dissatisfied because we have little idea of what is actually ours. We blow an inheritance that we did not need to touch, while returning to the Father hoping for crumbs instead of being accepted as sons. When we grasp the heart of the Father and what it is we've got, we'll never want to leave home. The wonderful thing is, as we live in love, we can go places and do things without home ever leaving us.

Failing to live like we belong will inevitably lead us to living like we don't belong. The *slave*, *squatter* and *searcher* lurk in every heart and that's why only truth can banish such thoughts of poverty and empower us to live, not as second-class citizens, but as sons.

My son snuggled because he knew he belonged. What do you know?

*"For you did not receive a spirit that makes you a slave again to fear, but you received the spirit of sonship. And by Him we cry, Abba Father."* (Romans 8:15)

# Chapter 8
# Soil of Success

"God carries your picture in His wallet."[1]

"When I look back on my childhood I wonder how I survived at all. It was, of course, a miserable childhood: the happy childhood is hardly worth your while. Worse than the ordinary miserable childhood is the miserable Irish childhood, and worse yet is the miserable Irish Catholic childhood.

People everywhere brag and whimper about the woes of their early years, but nothing can compare with the Irish version: the poverty; the shiftless loquacious alcoholic father; the pious defeated mother moaning by the fire; pompous priests; bullying schoolmasters; the English and the terrible things they did to us for eight hundred long years. Above all – we were wet."[2]

These are among the opening words of Frank McCourt's memoirs of his childhood, entitled *Angela's Ashes*. Though sprinkled with humour and filled with stories that prove the maxim "life is stranger than fiction" I reached the final page of the book asking myself the question, "How did Frank and his brothers survive?"

---

1. Tony Campolo.
2. McCourt, F., *Angela's Ashes*, UK, 1996, p.1.

Struggle lurks on every page and it feels like every character, from his relatives to the teachers and even the priest had more reason to be angry than happy. Frank's mother, Angela, is a constant throughout the book, but as I read, I was struck by his love for his father and the longing in his heart for intimacy with Malachy McCourt, his hero. He described his father like the Holy Trinity, "with three people in him". There was "the one in the morning with the paper, the one at night with the stories and the prayers, and then the one who does the bad thing and comes home with the smell of whiskey and wants us to die for Ireland".[3]

In Frank's world, boys weren't allowed to tell their fathers they loved them, nor fathers their sons for that matter. They could express this sentiment to God, babies and horses that win, "but anything else is a softness in the head". When his father left Ireland for England with the intention of earning money for the family, Frank could not have known that neither his father nor his money would ever return. I felt the pain of this moment as his hero disappeared, leaving all who depended on him in destitution. This event marked Frank as he grew. It was something he would never forget and would struggle to recover from.

If God is love, then everything He does towards us is motivated and governed by His love. If this is so, then it is His heart's desire that those on whom His love is focused know success, growth and life as He intended. If we conclude that God is love and He loves us, then we must also conclude that everything within Him is geared towards our wellbeing and the ultimate destiny of conforming us into the image of His Son, Jesus! Our Father does not merely want to fertilize the soil of our lives with love, rather He wants the soil itself to be love, out of which we blossom in strength, beauty and

---

3. Ibid., p.239. The "bad thing" was when his father would get unemployment benefit, *the dole*, and promptly drink it in the pub.

prosperity to become all that we should be. A sprinkle of love will not do it. If we are to grow strong and live well, our roots must be planted in love, drawing from its very essence and allowing its power to pulse through every facet of our lives.

Some people, like Frank McCourt, survive and even become successful in spite of their circumstances. Looking at his beginning we marvel he even made it. However, God's original plan was not that we "get through" in spite of what is going on around us. Rather, His intention has always been that men and women would thrive, increase and enjoy life out of the soil of success.

I love the imagery and beauty of the Song of Solomon/Songs (most men do!) Surrounded by controversy when the original Canon of Scripture was formed, there was great debate as to whether this book should even be included.[4] I'm glad it was. Saturated with intimacy, sensuous imagery and unrestrained passion, the Song draws us into the hearts of two lovers, totally consumed with each other. If the opening lines don't grab us, I'm not sure anything will:

*"Let him kiss me with the kisses of his mouth –*
*for your love is more delightful than wine."*
(Song of Songs 1:2)

That's it... I'm hooked. Tell me more. Due to the Church's unease with all things sexual, this book has suffered from over-spiritualization, but at heart it is an erotic love poem, capturing the words of two people, dizzy on the perfume of love and drunk on its wine.

As I read this delightful book, I learned some lessons about love and the soil of success.

---

4. The Canon is regarded as the complete body of inspired Scripture. The basic meaning of the word is a straight rod or rule, used as a measuring instrument.

*"He has taken me to the banquet hall, and his banner over me is love."* (Song of Songs 2:4)

**There is no-one like you!**
A group of people were asked about the greatest gift they'd ever received. A young successful lawyer said, "The greatest gift I ever had was a gift I received one Christmas. My dad gave me a small box. Inside was a note saying, 'Son, this year I will give you 365 hours – an hour every day after dinner. It's yours. We'll talk about what you want to talk about, we'll go where you want to go, play what you want to play. It will be your hour!'"

"My dad not only kept his promise," he said, "but every year he renewed it and it's the greatest gift I ever had in my life. I am the result of his time."

*"Like a lily among thorns, is my darling among the maidens."* (Song of Songs 2:2)

The lover in the story acknowledges the presence of other women, but sees his beloved as standing out from the rest – radiant, beautiful and special. If we assume the lover was King Solomon, it would have been difficult for him not to see other women – his world was literally surrounded by them. But now, in this instance, one woman stands out. In his eyes and there is no-one like her; she is special.

Did you know that you are special? Though the Bible declares that God has no favourites, it is also clear that those loved of God are special to Him, all of them. In an amazing way, in the economy of God's love, each of us stands out as special to our Father. He knows us and sees us as no-one else sees us.

I remember going to watch my eldest daughter Elaina perform in her first dancing show. She was one performer among dozens of young girls and a few boys. When she was on the stage, she never danced alone; at no time was the spotlight only on her... and yet, throughout the performance, which lasted a couple of hours, my eyes were continually drawn to her. She was special and she was mine. All the girls danced well, but when Elaina was on stage, I didn't notice anyone else.

*"My lover is mine and I am his..."* (Song of Songs 2:16)

Did you know you are His?

Did you know that He has no-one quite like you?

Did you know that you are special?

This is the power of love. When our lives are rooted in the soil of love, a consequence of such positioning and understanding is that we live with the knowledge that we are special, and that no-matter where we go, or how many are in the crowd, His eye is on us.

### The kiss will always fit

Dr Robert Seizer, in his book *Mortal Lessons: Notes in the Art of Surgery*, tells a remarkable story of performing surgery to remove a tumour in which it was necessary to sever a facial nerve, leaving a young woman's mouth permanently twisted. The Doctor's words say it all:

"Her young husband is in the room. He stands on the opposite side of the bed and together they seem to dwell in the evening lamplight, isolated from me, private. Who are they, I ask myself, he and this wry-mouth I have made, who gaze at and touch each other so generously, greedily? The young woman speaks. 'Will my mouth always be like this?' 'Yes,' I say, 'it will. It is because the nerve was cut.' She nods, and is silent. But the young man smiles, 'I like it,' he says. 'It is kind of cute.' All at once I know who he is. I understand, and I lower my gaze. One is not bold in an encounter with God. Unmindful, he bends to kiss her crooked mouth, and I, so close, can see how he twists his own lips to accommodate to hers, to show her that their kiss still works."[5]

I remember speaking at a seminar on issues related to marriage and love. I didn't just want to speak at people so, to open the session, I asked the question, "What do you most want from your marriage?" Everyone was a little nervous, looking round to see who would be brave enough to speak. After a few seconds (although it seemed a lot longer), a lady raised her hand. She had been married for many years and I will never forget her words.

"More than anything else, I want security. To know that I am loved and that this fact will never change. Women can endure a lot of things, but insecurity is not one of them. We need security and we thrive when we have it."

*"His left arm is under my head and his right arm embraces me."*
(Song of Songs 2:6)

What a picture of security this is. The young woman lies in the embrace and protection of her lover. She is not concerned about any other issue at this moment. For a few seconds the worries, demands and pressures of her life are forgotten; she rests in the arms of her lover, secure in his physical embrace and secure in the knowledge that she is loved. Every one of us needs to know that we are secure, that we are loved, and that this fact won't change. To wake up each day and wonder if God still loves us, if He's in a good mood, or if by chance He's changed His mind would induce such a level of insecurity as to cripple us and stunt our growth. We cannot live truly successful lives unless we are secure.

5. John, J., & Stibbe, M., *A Box of Delights*, UK, 2001, p.109.

Though the Bible makes it clear that God is love and that this amazing fact won't change, many people live in their own reality, believing, "This can't be true and any minute now God will renege on His end of the deal." As we've seen already, this produces insecurity, which infects a person's mind, worship and service. How can we love Him if we aren't sure He loves us? How can we worship Him when we do it from a premise of uncertainty? How can we serve Him when insecurity saturates our belief system?

The story is told of a man who, as a boy, never felt affirmed by his father and lived in a world dominated by insecurity. As the boy became a man he realised that his father's critical spirit made him wonder if he had ever been accepted as a son. He was in his mid-forties and married with children of his own when one day his father, whom he had not seen for five years, telephoned to say he was about to visit. He panicked. He now had a beard and he knew his father would not approve. The old man was due to arrive in five days time and on each of those days the son argued with himself over whether or not he should shave off his beard.

He found himself talking to himself: *"You're a father yourself now. You must make your own decisions."* But at ten o'clock on the morning of the day his father was due to arrive, he shaved off his beard. He waited on a crowded platform and suddenly saw his father walking towards him. He smiled and went to shake his father's hand, but hesitated as he saw the old man's brow furrow. His father said, "Nice to see you son. But aren't those sideburns a little long?" At that moment he knew that nothing had changed. This was still the man he could not please.

Insecurity will force a destructive wedge between our Father and us, but this is not His heart. He wants nothing to get in between His embrace and ours. He wants us to experience first hand the benefits of being planted in the soil of love, the life of which will naturally produce the fruit of security and freedom. He wants us to know that no matter what happens, His kiss will always fit!

## You are always on my mind

On the day that *America told the truth*, an incredible statistic emerged about infidelity. Almost one-third of those married Americans questioned (31%) said they had engaged in or were currently having affairs. The majority of those questioned were not just one-night stands; on average, most affairs were lasting almost a year. Driven by the philosophy "everybody else is doing it", a staggering 62% of Americans believed that there was nothing morally wrong with having affairs. The great majority of men and women having affairs firmly believe that other married men and women do the same. Most women questioned liked their lovers better than their husbands, while the reverse was true for men: they liked their wives better! So why do it?

The reasons given for having affairs ranged from the naïve to the ridiculous. 28% said it was due to a "casual meeting" while 12% said "it just happened, it was an accident." 10% put it down to a "growing friendship" and 7% said it was due to being "introduced by a friend". 7% concluded it was "sexual attraction" while 7% put it down to "being pursued" by their eventual lover. 3% succumbed to an "old flame", while a sad 2% blamed it on a "mid-life crisis".[6]

"It's not my fault I cheated on my wife/husband... I have an excuse!" All of the above may indeed be accepted as legitimate reasons why affairs happen, but are they the real reasons? It's a complex issue, I know, but I have a theory. If each of the people questioned had invested the same amount of energy into the

---

6. Patterson & Kim, op.cit., pp.94-99.

relationship they had with their husband or wife – if this had been their priority and they had lived in the realm of satisfaction with the one they had vowed their lives to – they would neither have had the time nor the inclination to cheat and stray. When love truly reigns, when we are rooted in the rich nutrients of its soil, the dynamic consequence of this is satisfaction, contentment and rest. Why would we want to go somewhere else, when we have everything we need here? Why should I invest in something or someone else, when my investment is needed here?

*"Like an apple tree among the trees of the forest is my lover among the young men. I delight to sit in his shade, and his fruit is sweet to my taste."* (Song of Songs 2:3)

Does she sound satisfied to you? With this level of customer satisfaction, he'll be the only thing on her mind.

If we can learn to live and walk in the love of God, we will enjoy the fruit of a satisfied life. People only want more because they aren't satisfied with what they have. God our Father has given so much, investing all of heaven into our success, and when we understand this then He will always be on our mind. That does not mean we will not think about other things, but He will be the dominant figure in our thinking, with no thought of infidelity or betrayal.

When the Apostle Paul was in prison, facing the certain threat of execution under Nero, he wrote a letter to his friends. It's among the last recorded words of Paul and in the Bible we call it 2 Timothy.

*"For Demas, because he loved this world, has deserted me and has gone to Thessalonica."* (2 Timothy 4:10)

Demas had been through hell and high water with Paul. Did he leave because it was tough? I don't think so, for it seems he was as tough as they come. He left because he fell in love with something else. In fact when he became dissatisfied with what he had the question was not, *will* he leave, but *when*? Dissatisfaction will soon have us walking out the door, but when love is the soil and we invest our lives into it as God has done, walking will never be an option. Oh, I didn't say temptation will never happen, but when we are tempted, if our roots are in the soil of love, if the love of the Father is satisfying our souls, then we won't do a Demas. Rather, we'll stay faithful and live in love's power right to the end.

## Fruit galore

Ever been strawberry picking? We have and we loved it. The smell of strawberries on your hands beats Chanel any day. The idea is to get a basket, go out into the field, fill it to the brim and then have the contents weighed before paying. My children, however, soon realised that *they* don't get weighed, so came up with the idea of eating while picking. Believe me, the words of the eighth commandment echoed in my head as I tried to stop my offspring eating any more of the forbidden fruit for fear of a sudden thunderbolt of destruction. However, have you ever tried to tell off a child for eating strawberries when the red juice is smudged all over their mouths, like poorly applied lipstick? And yes, they smile that smile. It's just too tempting for children (and adults) when a field is so laden with fruit. Later we enjoyed those strawberries with ice-cream, cream, and a sprinkling of chocolate on the top. A healthy plant, set in good rich soil is a vital combination for producing glorious, abundant crops. The fruit is the natural consequence of both of these factors coming together (and a few more, I understand). We cannot hope to grow great fruit from deficient soil. It is impossible.

*"But my own vineyard is mine to give; the thousand shekels are for you, O Solomon..."* (Song of Songs 8:12)

Solomon owned a vineyard and let it out to tenants. As a result they would pay him, from the fruit harvested, the sum of a thousand shekels as part of the agreement. However, his beloved owned her own vineyard and not only did it produce excellent fruit, but she voluntarily yielded it to her lover, drawn to do so by the love she had for him. Out of love, she gave an abundant harvest of fruit. We cannot live in love, enjoy its soil and not begin to produce. A natural consequence of living in love is the fruit of love and a harvest of life-fruit, manifest in attitudes, life-choices and lifestyle. I passionately believe that if you want to see how much a man loves his wife, don't listen to him, look at her. The evidence of his love will be manifest in the harvest of her life. If he loves her as much as he claims, then everyone will identify the fruit of such love in her lifestyle. If we claim to live in God's love, knowing and understanding what He has deposited into the soil in which we grow, then the evidence will be seen by all in our lifestyle.

David talked of the righteous being like a planted tree. For the man who delights in God and His Word, David proclaimed:

*"He is like a tree planted by streams of water, which yields its fruit in season and whose leaf does not wither. Whatever he does prospers."* (Psalm 1:3)

Similar language is used in a later psalm when David writes,

*"The righteous will flourish like a palm tree, they will grow like a cedar of Lebanon; planted in the house of the Lord, they will flourish in the courts of our God. They will still bear fruit in old age, they will stay fresh and green, proclaiming, 'The Lord is upright; He is my Rock, and there is no wickedness in Him.'"* (Psalm 92:12-15)

LOVED

The result of getting properly planted in the right soil and feeding on the right nutrients is that we produce fruit worthy of the soil. If we proclaim to the world that God is love and that we live in His love, surely one of the results should be fruit that shows the world the value of being planted in such soil. If our fruit is no better than theirs, if our lives are as weak as theirs, if what we produce is as poor as what they produce, then how can we proclaim the value of the soil in which we are planted? The person planted in God produces fruit of high quality. Their lives reflect the extraordinary nature of the soil in which they are planted. They proclaim to the world the awesomeness of God's love through the magnificence of the fruit they produce. Theirs is the fruit of love from the soil of success.

The success of our lives should not be in spite of the soil in which we stand, but because of it. God has not planted us and abandoned us to make it on our own. He plants us where we will have every chance of becoming all that we should be. He has planted us in His love, which has the power to change everything and create a springboard from which we can live outstanding lives. I love how Ray Bevan put it: "As I look back on my life, I can see that one of the most important lessons I have learned is that I am special, I am important; I am a unique individual with a unique destiny to discover. I am not an accident; I am not the result of sex or of people – they were just the means to get me here. My real sense of value comes from the knowledge that God knew me before I was even in my mother's womb, and my days were written for me; waiting for me to live them, even before that."[7]

Get planted and stay planted in the soil of success.

7. Bevan, R., *Prepared for Greatness*, UK, 2004, p.xi.

# Chapter 9
# Fear's Greatest Fear

"Give yourself up with joy to a loving confidence in God and
have courage to believe firmly that God's action toward you is a
masterpiece of partiality and love.
Rest tranquilly in this abiding conviction."[1]

"What girl does not love her father? A father is a big tree sheltering
the family, the beams that support a house, the guardian of his
wife and children. But I don't love my father – I hate him."

On the year Hongxue turned eleven, her father started to
abuse her. Seeking to conceal his crime, he told his daughter,
"Your mother has never liked you... if she finds out I love you
this much she will want even less to do with you." As the abuse
continued, it grew steadily worse, not just happening under the
cover of darkness, but at virtually any opportunity. On more
than one occasion the child was attacked when her mother was
cooking in the next room or had left to go to the toilet. Life
became unbearable for the young woman. Writing to a friend she
confessed, "I became more and more afraid of 'this' love." Her
father's "love" turned to anger and hatred, threatening her if she
ever told anyone and branding her a "broken shoe".

---

1. Abbe Henri de Tourville.

Fear began to dominate her. She feared going to sleep, being alone, spending time at home or being around her father. As a result of her treatment, she fell ill and hoped to find relief in hospital, but even there it continued, with her father taking advantage of her weakened state, even defiling her hospital bed. Her words illuminate her terrified and broken heart during this period: "I could not stop crying. Was this my father? Had he had children just to satisfy his animal lusts? What had he given life to me for?"

This pattern of living continued over the next couple of years. Incredibly, the young woman recounts how she found comfort from a fly. "A dear little fly once showed me the touch of loving hands," she wrote. Longing for the love of a father and mother, such was her destitution that the child found solace from an insect. "Because I long for a real mother and father: a real family where I can be a child, and cry in my parents' arms; where I can sleep safely in my bed at home; where loving hands will stroke my head to comfort me after a bad dream. From my earliest childhood, I have never felt this love. I hoped and yearned for it, but I have never had it, and I will never have it now..." On 11th September 1975, the young woman died of septicaemia. The infection which eventually killed her had been caused by a fly, which this lonely victim of a "father's love" had squashed into a cut in her arm.[2]

When I read Hongxue's story I was deeply upset. I have two beautiful daughters and a handsome son. Knowing the life they have, in a home where they are loved and cherished, I cannot imagine the suffering of this lovely little girl, forced to be a woman before her time. The hands that should have nurtured her to life and maturity doomed her to impoverishment and a premature

---

2. Xinran, *The Good Woman of China*, 2002, pp.9-33. Hongxue's story is told under the chapter heading, *The Girl Who Kept a Fly as a Pet.*

death. She died in the most fearful of all places this side of hell: alone and unloved.

John tells us,

*"There is no fear in love. But perfect love drives out fear, because fear has to do with punishment. The one who fears is not made perfect in love."* (1 John 4:18)

There is only one thing that fear fears and that is love, for there is no place like love. Ask a child snuggled into the arms of a parent, ask the woman in the embrace of her man, or ask the dad racing to get home after a trip away. Listen to the one overwhelming cry of injured and dying men on a battlefield, "Mother."

I'm not sure what I was expecting on a cold Friday night in Doncaster when I joined a team to minister to the *street girls*, but the young woman standing in front of me didn't look like a prostitute. In another place at another time, she could have been a mother, sister, wife and friend. But there she was, selling her body on a freezing Friday night, to feed her habit to stay alive. She hadn't always been like this. A lifetime ago she had a job, a strong relationship and her own home, but stuff had happened and this was now her life. As we offered her hot chocolate and something to eat she asked in her strong Scottish accent, "Why are you people doing this? Why are you here wasting your time on the likes of me?" Before I could open my mouth, Teresa, my friend answered, "We're here because we love you." There was no judgement in her voice, just sincere unadulterated love. "Rachel" was clearly moved, tears welling up in her beautiful eyes. She grasped her cup of hot chocolate like her life depended on it and as she did so, Teresa noticed how cold her gloveless hands looked. In a moment of intimate tenderness, Teresa removed her thick woollen gloves and offered them to Rachel. After a short protest the young prostitute put the gloves on and spoke words

I'll never forget, "These gloves are wonderful, they feel so warm." That night Rachel would experience anything but warmth from the punters circling her like sharks with the smell of blood in the water. However, for a moment, she felt how good love could be in the warm gloves of a friend.

*There is no place like love.* It's the place in which God designed us to live. Every one of us need it, deep down we want it, and the truth is, it is God's desire to lavish it on us. Fear will always attempt to drive us away from the love of God, from the God who is love. However, the incredible truth is, if we allow His love to get close to us, if we dare to take up the offer of putting our hands into His warm gloves, His love will drive the fear away! Fear tells us we are not loved and that only judgement and condemnation await those who attempt to get close to God, but love tells a different story. Love takes us to a place where we are accepted, appreciated and adored. Love lifts us to the understanding that we are in fact the apple of God's eye; that our names are inscribed on the palm of His hand; and that come hell or high water, He will always love us. This is fear's greatest fear: that one day our hearts will discover the one thing that has the power to destroy it: *Love!*

## Love is a peace-maker

*"There is no fear in love. But perfect love drives out fear..."*

Fear is a terrible thing, ravenously destructive and mercilessly efficient. Its ambition is to master the world in which it lives and when it invades our heart it is with the ambition of total domination. There is no thought of "power-sharing" or compromise – it wants to rule. Fear looks for hearts where love does not live, knowing they are the easiest targets. With the walls broken down and undefended, fear can sweep unopposed into the kingship of our lives.

The word John uses here points to fear having the ability to "put to flight, to flee" or put another way, to scare away; to get our hearts and minds on the run. Once we start running because of fear, it's very hard to stop.

My grandfather fought in World War II with the 36<sup>th</sup> Ulster Gunner Division in the Burma conflict. So accurate was his unit that they were given the nickname "The twelve-mile snipers". However, before my grandfather even entered the war, he had to be trained, part of which took place in London. It was there he met up with a Sergeant Major who was determined to make their lives hell. He cursed at them, beat them, criticised them and labelled them "worthless Irish scum, fit for nothing but dying". It was his job to make fighting men out of them and, I'm guessing, his methods were more stick than carrot. When my grandfather's unit eventually made it to Burma, it wasn't long before they were engaged in their first conflict against fierce, battle-hardened Japanese fighters. When the fighting stopped and a head-count was made of those alive, injured or dead, the Sergeant Major could not be found. He had done a runner. Fear had gripped his heart and he could not stand it. He knew the theory of war, but had never actually experienced it. Fear was king and he ran for his life. My grandfather never saw or heard of him again!

This is the power of fear. Once it gets inside, it can get us on the run and leave us destitute. Where fear is king, insecurity reigns and we avoid the One who claims to love us. Praise becomes like penitence, devotion becomes merely a matter of duty, and faith is a joyless, lifeless experience.

However, John doesn't leave it there. He tells us,

"... *perfect love drives out fear.*"

The word used here can literally mean "to turn out-of-doors".

In other words, to kick it out of your house! When love and fear collide we truly have the clash of the Titans, for both seek to reign and both have the power to drive lesser opponents from the scene of battle. Love that is complete and reigns in our lives by faith has the power to drive fear from our hearts. Love doesn't just joust with fear, sparring to see who wins. One punch from love and it's all over. When we walk in a clear revelation of the God of love and how much we are loved, fear will not even be able to find a small hole in the ground in which to hide. Fear is banished from the land where love is king!

Are you afraid?

I encourage you to invite love into the landscape of your life. Get into the Word and discover what God says about you and the extent to which He loves you. If fear dominates, it will drive all love, joy, peace and hope from your heart. Fear will take you far from home and keep you on the run until the day you die. Love is the cure, the peacemaker, the powerful antidote to the evil of fear. Living in the knowledge that you are loved is the key to living as a conqueror over the power of fear.

What reigns: love or fear?

### Love is a confidence-giver

*"... because fear has to do with punishment."*

A story is told about a soldier who came home after fighting in the Vietnam War. He called his parents from San Francisco. "Mom and Dad, I'm coming home, but I've a favour to ask. I have a friend I'd like to bring home with me." "Sure," they replied, "we'd love to meet him." "There's something you should know," the son continued. "He was hurt pretty badly in the fighting. He stepped on a land mine and lost an arm and a leg. He has nowhere else to go, and I want him to come live with us." "I'm sorry to hear that son. Maybe we can help him find somewhere to live." "No, Mom and Dad, I want him to live with us." "Son," said the father, "you don't know what you're asking. Someone with such a handicap would be a terrible burden on us. We have our own lives to live, and we can't let something like this interfere with our lives. I think you should just come home and forget about this guy. He'll find a way to live on his own."

At that point the son hung up the phone. The parents heard nothing more from him until a few days later they received a phone call from the San Francisco police. They were told their son had died after falling from a building and the police believed it was suicide. The grief-stricken parents flew to San Francisco and were taken to the city morgue to identify the body of their son. They recognized him, but to their horror they also discovered something they didn't know: their son had only one arm and one leg.[3]

Fear will always rob us of the confidence and the security to come home. An expectation of punishment and lack of confidence in our acceptance before God will produce fear. If we are not convinced God is for us, that He loves and is committed to us, then there will always be a nagging doubt, which is both fed by and feeds fear. Lack of confidence in who God is and who we are produces the opportunity for fear to invade. Once encamped, fear exploits the weakness of insecurity already present and drives a wedge between us and the presence of God. The ignorance which allows fear to reign locks us into an expectation of punishment, when the truth is only love awaits. The only answer to ignorance is knowledge of the truth, and holding to that when fear probes the walls for weaknesses.

---

3. John, J., & Stibbe, M., *A Bucket of Surprises*, UK, 2002, p.110.

*"And I pray that you, being rooted and established in love, may have the power, together with all the saints, to grasp how wide and long and high and deep is the love of Christ, and to know this love that surpasses knowledge – that you may be filled to the measure of all the fullness of God."* (Ephesians 3:17-19)

We've touched on this verse already, but we need to remind ourselves of its truth. The dimensions of God's love for us are huge and even when we grasp it by revelation it is still beyond our knowing. Engaging with this love will drive away fear and dispel the expectation of punishment, allowing us to live in the freedom of His love, not to please ourselves, but to please Him.

Ignorance says that we are condemned, but the truth about love says:

*"Therefore, there is now no condemnation for those who are in Christ Jesus."* (Romans 8:1)

Ignorance says that we cannot approach God, He does not love or want us, we are second class citizens, but the truth about love says:

*"Let us approach the throne of grace with confidence, so that we may receive mercy and find grace to help us in our time of need."* (Hebrews 4:16)

The power of love releases us from uncertainty and the expectation of punishment and leads us to a place where we can come to God, not arrogantly (for He hates this) but confidently, secure in the knowledge of who He is and His love for us. If love reigns it will produce a confidence within us to live, worship and serve. There will be no nagging doubts or an expectation of rejection. We will live with our heads up and approach our God with the revelation that we are loved and that the ground of love is totally, unshakeably secure.

Fear's greatest fear is that you live in the knowledge of God's love.

## Love is a life-changer

*"The one who fears is not made perfect in love."*

The word "perfect" used in this phrase is a very interesting one. It is often used to describe men who are full grown, of full age and mature. It carries the idea of something being brought to its end or finished, and needing nothing necessary to bring it to completeness. Perfect in this context does not mean without fault or defect, rather it points to wholeness, completeness and maturity. When we find the place of love, when we understand the power of love, we move to a place of completeness in ourselves and to maturity beyond our experience. Yes, we will always be learning and growing, but having come to know His love, we are in fact complete. The presence of fear in our lives, in relation to the love of God, shows that we have not yet reached maturity regarding His love. This has little to do with the maturity of years or how long we've followed Jesus – rather it is to do with receiving a revelation of His love, which produces in us rest and wholeness. The amazing fact is a child can grasp this truth, have fear driven from their heart and be "perfect", complete in God's love. On the other hand, someone may have followed Jesus for many years and still struggle with fear in the context of their relationship with the Father. Though loved, they are incomplete and live as such.

In 1 Corinthians 13, Paul outlines seventeen distinct attributes of love.

*"Love is patient, love is kind. It does not envy, it does not boast, it is not proud. It is not rude, it is not self-seeking, it is not easily angered, it keeps no records of wrongs. Love does not delight in*

*evil but rejoices with the truth. It always protects, always trusts, always hopes, always perseveres. Love never fails."* (v4-8)

Although written to the Corinthian church in the context of human relationships and behaviour, this snapshot of love shows us something of the magnificence of our God and the rules of love which govern how He lives and behaves towards us.

Paul goes on,

*"... but when perfection comes, the imperfect disappears. When I was a child, I talked like a child, I thought like a child, I reasoned like a child. When I became a man I put childish ways behind me."* (v10-11)

There is much debate on what this means. Many believe there is a future aspect to these words, a completion that points to the ultimate appearing of Jesus and the consummation of all things here on earth, and verse 12 seems to bear this out. However, could it be that in the context of calling love "the most excellent way" and the greatest of the three that remain (faith and hope being the other two), Paul was pointing to a perfection that is ours when we truly grasp the knowledge of His love that surpasses knowledge and live in its power. He's no longer thinking like a child, he understands some of the great issues of love and life now, and this has brought him to a greater sense of completeness. Will the imperfect only vanish when we stand in heaven, or is it possible to live in the perfection of His love, today?

The reason love is fear's greatest fear is because it moves us from immaturity to maturity. It transforms us from being childish in our thinking, limited and narrow, to truly understanding what is really going on. Fear is terrified by the perfection of love, for once we learn to live there, we are complete and as far as fear is concerned, we are invincible. Fear has no weapon in its armoury strong enough to threaten or combat love. A boxer once proclaimed to the world that he was the greatest. He could float like a butterfly and sting like a bee. Paul declares love to be the greatest, because only love has the power to deal fear the knockout punch.

A young boy came upon an old man who was fishing in the mighty Mississippi River. Immediately, he began to ask the old fisherman lots of questions, as only young boys can do. With the patience of a saint, he answered every one of the lad's questions. Suddenly, their conversation was interrupted by the shrill whistle of the majestic River Queen paddling relentlessly down river. The sight of the ship gleaming and splashing spray in the sunlight caused the surprised spectators to stare in awe and appreciation. Then above the noise of the paddle wheel, the boy's voice was heard calling across the water, "Let me ride! Let me ride!" The old man turned to the boy and tried to calm him down, explaining that the River Queen was too important a ship to stop and give rides to little boys. But the boy cried all the more, "Let me ride!"

Old eyes bulged in disbelief as the great ship pulled for shore and a gangplank was lowered. In a flash the boy scampered up onto the plank. With its new cargo on board the River Queen began to pull back into the main stream, the old man continuing to stare. Suddenly the boy appeared at the rail and shouted, *"Mister, I knew this ship would stop for me. The captain is my dad!"*

It will amaze us how differently we live when we know the Captain is our Dad. The knowledge of His love and the power that His love produces in us is the one thing above all that fear fears. But the perfect love John spoke of is a peacemaker, confidence-giver and a life-changer. Our Father wants us to live in a fear-free zone, and the only way that will happen is if we live in the power of His love.

Fear's greatest fear is that we realise *the Captain is our Dad* for it knows such love-knowledge will drive the fear away. Start living like you're loved.

# Chapter 10
# The Laughter of Love

"The supreme happiness of life is the conviction that we are
loved."[1]

A friend of mine sent me the following metaphors, which
apparently came from actual answers written by young people
during GCSE examination essays.

- The little boat gently drifted across the pond exactly the way
  a bowling ball wouldn't.
- Her hair glistened in the rain like nose hair after a sneeze.
- He was as tall as a six-foot-three-inch tree.
- John and Mary had never met. They were like two
  hummingbirds who had also never met.
- The young fighter had a hungry look, the kind you get from
  not eating for a while.
- He was a lame duck. Not the metaphorical lame duck either,
  but a real duck that was actually lame. Maybe from stepping
  on a land mine or something.
- She had a deep, throaty, genuine laugh, like that sound a dog
  makes just before it throws up.

---

1. Victor Hugo.

- It was a working class tradition, like fathers chasing kids around with their power tools.
- He was deeply in love. When she spoke, he thought he heard bells, as if she were a dustcart reversing.
- She walked into my office like a centipede with 98 missing legs.

Just one more, my personal favourite:

- It hurt the way your tongue hurts after you accidentally staple it to the wall!

Your body should now be performing what the *Encyclopaedia Britannica* describes as "rhythmic, vocalized, expiratory and involuntary actions" – or put another way, laughing. It's that moment when "fifteen facial muscles contract and stimulation of the zygomatic major muscle (the main lifting mechanism of your upper lip) occurs. Meanwhile, the respiratory system is upset by the epiglottis half-closing the larynx so that air intake occurs irregularly, making you gasp. In extreme circumstances, the tear ducts are activated, so that while the mouth is opening and closing and the struggle for oxygen intake continues, the face becomes moist and often red (or purple). The noises that usually accompany this bizarre behaviour range from sedate giggles to boisterous guffaws."[2]

After reading that explanation, you're probably not laughing any more... sorry!

The Bible says;

*"A cheerful heart is good medicine, but a crushed spirit dries up the bones."* (Proverbs 17:22)

---

2. www.howstuffworks.com/laughter

I believe laughter is a fruit of love. When we know we're loved, when we are confident in our position as children of God and the lengths our Father has gone to demonstrate His love to us, then we will learn to laugh and laugh well. Laughter is not only compatible with love, it's inseparable from it. We can laugh without being loved, but we cannot live in the revelation that we are loved and not laugh.

Laughter is the hallmark of the loved!

## Who is that?

When I was a child I remember watching a movie called *The Greatest Story Ever Told*. It's an epic portrayal of the life of Jesus from birth to ascension. As a youngster I was awestruck by it and transfixed by Jesus, played by the actor Max Von Sydow. What a movie, I thought! A few years ago I had the opportunity to watch it again. I settled down on a lazy Easter holiday afternoon with my nibbles and a glass of Pepsi, prepared to be wowed all over again. As the film progressed, I became more and more disillusioned. I kept asking myself, "Who is that?" I knew the central character was supposed to be Jesus. He had the white robe, the flowing long hair and the beard, but where was the smile? Where was the passion? Where was the zest for life? This guy was so boring and miserable I wouldn't have followed him to the end of the street, never mind the ends of the earth. What had happened to Jesus? In one scene Jesus was teaching the beatitudes: "Blessed are the poor in spirit… blessed are they that mourn… blessed…" but he seemed to be forcing the words through clenched teeth, with an expression that suggested he was about to pass a kidney stone. Do you know what blessed means?

*Happy*!

Unfortunately, this is how many see Jesus, even those who follow Him: totally serious and totally boring. I ask you, would children want to be around a guy like that? Would you want your children to be around a man like that? Can you imagine Jesus at a wedding? There He is, sitting in the corner, contemplating some deep, profound truth while everyone else drinks the good wine, dances and enjoys the celebration. I don't think so! I reckon Jesus was a great dancer. I think He was the life and soul of the party and knew the difference between the dregs of the barrel and the quality grapes. Oh, don't get me wrong, He never ran to excess; He lived a life that reflected the glory and majesty of heaven, holy and sinless. But He knew how to laugh and have fun.

Why don't we laugh more in Church? Why aren't Christians known as fun people to be around? What's gone wrong?

Following God is serious, but serious doesn't mean a lack of laughter and joy. It is possible to live a purposeful, focused and radical life while still having fun, enjoying the journey and laughing a lot on the way. God expects it and has built laughter into the fabric of love. He wants us to be joyous advertisements for the Kingdom of God. The Bible has a lot of positive stuff to say about laughter and joy, but the problem is, over the years we've tended to zero in on the negative bits. Our preoccupation with the colour black, hard pews, cold buildings and hell-fire sermons probably hasn't helped the Church sell the message that life is about enjoyment. I suggest that if a PR consultant was called to help the Church connect with society, changing the perception that Christianity is joyless and irrelevant might be at the top of their "To-do" list. Those who love misery do get some solace from the Bible. Solomon in the Book of Ecclesiastes wrote,

*"Laughter is foolish..."* and later added, *"Sorrow is better than laughter, because a sad face is good for the heart."* (Ecclesiastes 2:2, 7:3).

These words not only contradict his own, contained in the book of Proverbs, but much of the balance of the Bible. We have to remember that the book of Ecclesiastes records the conclusions of a man making a journey from disillusionment to life. The opening line of the book is enough to suggest he's having a hard time. Some of Solomon's words in this book are *wrong*, and some of his conclusions are *incorrect*, but they are recorded for our learning. We need to remember that not every sentence in the Bible expresses what God says or thinks! Solomon was living a purposeless, joyless life, disconnected from a vibrant, living relationship with God. He's grasping for truth and satisfaction, and struggling through much misery.

Those that have found love, know love, and live in love, should be people who reflect the *joy of love*. Laughter will be our hallmark and not far from our language. Like everyone, we have challenges and upsets, but out of our *lovedness* we learn to laugh. The Church should be a place that is familiar with the sound of laughter and Christians should be people who know how to laugh. "Such infectiously joyful believers have no trouble convincing people around them that Christianity is real and that Christ can transform a life. Joy is the flag that flies above the castle of their hearts, announcing that the King is in residence."[3]

When I read the following story it moved me to tears and motivated me to chill out a little and laugh more. "In church the other Sunday I was intent on a small child who was turning around smiling at everyone. He wasn't gurgling, spitting, humming, kicking, tearing the hymnals or rummaging through his mother's

---

3. Swindoll, C., *Laugh Again*, USA, 1991, p.7.

handbag. He was just smiling. Finally, his mother jerked him about and in a stage whisper that could be heard in a little theatre off Broadway said, 'Stop that grinning! You're in church!' With that, she gave him a belt and as the tears rolled down his cheeks added, 'That's better,' and returned to her prayers. Suddenly I was angry. It occurred to me the entire world is in tears... I wanted to grab this child with the tear-stained face close to me and tell him about my God. The happy God. The smiling God. The God who had to have a sense of humour to have created the likes of us... What a fool I thought. Here was a woman sitting next to the only light left in our civilization – the only hope, our only miracle – our only promise of infinity. If he couldn't smile in church, where was there left to go?"[4]

"Cheerfulness is no sin, nor is there any grace in a solemn cast of countenance."[5]

Hopefully, when people hear laughter they'll ask, "Who is that?" and someone will answer, "Oh, that's the Church!"

**What makes you laugh?**
Yes, we've even got theories on this. There are three basic theories on what makes us laugh.

The *incongruity theory* suggests that humour arises when logic and familiarity are replaced by things that don't normally go together. Researcher Thomas Veatch says a joke becomes funny when we expect one outcome and another happens.

The *superiority theory* comes into play when we laugh at jokes that focus on someone else's mistakes, stupidity or misfortune. We feel superior to this person, experience a certain detachment from the situation, and so are able to laugh at it.

4. Yancey, op.cit., quoting humourist Erma Bombeck's column, p.32.
5. John Newton.

THE LAUGHTER OF LOVE

The *relief theory* is the basis for a device moviemakers have used effectively for a long time. In action films or thrillers where tension is high, the director uses comic relief at just the right time. He builds up the tension or suspense as much as possible and then breaks it down slightly with a side comment, enabling the viewer to relieve himself of pent-up emotion, just so the movie can build it up again![6]

Different things make different people laugh, and if our laughter is based on external influences alone, then our joy has more to do with what is happening around us and to us than with what exists within us. Lots of things can make us laugh, but if the only time we laugh is when we see or hear or experience something funny, then we are missing a vital piece of the laughter picture.

*"A happy heart makes the face cheerful, but heartache crushes the spirit."* (Proverbs 15:13)

The source of our smiles must not be reduced to the brilliance of a comedian or a scene in a movie; it must go much deeper than that. These things can inspire laughter, but only the heart can make us laugh. If the heart is healthy and whole, we'll laugh a lot more. If the heart is broken or sick, though we may smile or even engage in the occasional chuckle, we won't laugh a lot.

For years the BBC ran a programme called *One Foot in the Grave*. I watched it once and then refused to ever watch it again. Life is hard enough without listening to the rantings of an unhappy, opinionated cynic – especially when I'm paying for the licence! The main character, Victor Meldrew, was continuously miserable. He was deeply unhappy and therefore could not understand how anyone else could or should be happy. Though he made many laugh, he rarely smiled himself. We can be surrounded by good people, great things and wonderful opportunities, but if the heart

---

6. www.howstuffworks.com

LOVED

is sick, we will struggle to laugh at all. Your face will only do what your heart tells it to, and if you're smiling on the inside, it will reach the outside.

Some may say, "Ah, but you don't understand, I'm a serious person." I believe Jesus was a serious person and for that matter I believe I am deeply serious about my life, but it's okay to laugh more. It's okay to give our heart some medicine and give our face a break, not to mention the people around us; allow the joy in our spirit to come out. We can laugh and be serious at the same time, it's not an either or situation. No-one was born serious, we learned to be that way. So if that's the case, it can be unlearned and new habits and beliefs learned.

*Well, I've nothing to laugh about.* That's because we don't understand where laughter comes from. Laughter doesn't come from a perfect marriage, angelic children or a huge bank balance (although I'm up for all of those things). If that were the case, most people I know could never laugh. Laughter doesn't just come from without, it primarily comes from within. Laughter doesn't come from circumstances, it comes from the condition of the heart.

"The happiest people are rarely the richest, or the most beautiful, or even the most talented. Happy people do not depend on excitement and 'fun'-supplied externals. They enjoy the fundamental, often very simple, things of life... Without exception, people who consistently laugh do so *in spite of*, seldom *because of* anything. They pursue fun rather than wait for it to knock on their door in the middle of the day."[7]

People who are living in the love of God have a different set of values and priorities. The events around them may indeed create a humourous situation, at which and with which they can laugh.

7. Swindoll, op.cit., p.7, my italics.

136

But, their laughter is not dependent on this, for their laughter comes from a loved heart, bursting with energy and health. Even when there's nothing to laugh about, they can be found with joy in their heart and a smile on their face. I'm not talking about 24/7, non-stop laughing, but rather a life where joy and laughter are never far away.

## The healthy option

In 1972, Dr. Hunter "Patch" Adams founded the *Gesundheit! Institute* in response, to what he saw as the health care crisis in America. Its mission statement reads,

"To bring fun, friendship and the joy of service back into health care."

In 1969 he voluntarily checked himself into a mental institution, unable to cope with the world around him. His life was full of pain and the future was bleak. While in the hospital he started helping some of the patients and discovered he not only enjoyed doing it, but he was good at it. He discharged himself and eventually signed up for medical school, where he was told that the humanity was to be trained out of him.

Patch Adams vigorously resisted this philosophy and secretly engaged with patients using some very unusual tactics, mostly involving humour. He challenged the system and out of it was born the vision for *Gesundheit!* which means "good health". The Institute is run on the belief that health is based on happiness. One of its selling points is that it is "much more than simply a medical center. The Gesundheit! facility will be a microcosm of life, integrating medical care with farming, arts and crafts, performing arts, education, nature, recreation, friendship and fun."[8]

---

8. www.patchadams.org

Patch Adams had discovered something in the late 1960s, which the Bible had talked about thousands of years before:

*"A cheerful heart is good medicine, but a crushed spirit dries up the bones."* (Proverbs 17:22)

This is now a medically proven fact! The medical profession have known for some time that laughter and happiness can be a major help in coping with illness and stress. But researchers are now saying that laughter can do a lot more. Their conclusion is that it can bring balance to all the components of the immune system, which of course helps fight off disease. Stress hormones suppress the immune system, increase the number of blood platelets (which can block arteries) and raise blood pressure. Laughter reduces levels of these stress hormones (those "fight or flight" responses which kick into action in our bodies when we experience stress, anger or hostility) and acts as a safety valve, shutting off their unnecessary flow.

Stay with me now... when we're laughing, natural killer cells that destroy tumours and viruses increase, as do Gamma-interferon (a disease fighting protein), T-cells, which are a major part of the immune response, and B-cells, which make disease destroying antibodies. What may further surprise us is that researchers estimate that laughing 100 times is equal to 10 minutes on a rowing machine or 15 minutes on an exercise bike. As we laugh, blood pressure is lowered and there is an increase in vascular blood flow and in oxygenation of the blood, which further assists healing. Laughter gives our diaphragm and abdominal, respiratory, facial, leg and back muscles a work out.[9] If you didn't get all that, here it is: laughter is the healthy option. As we laugh, it is literally doing us good. It's worth having a laugh just for that, don't you think?

---

9. www.howstuffworks.com

Imagine, not just laughing when funny things get to you but learning to laugh as part of your lifestyle. Imagine living in such rest and in such an understanding of our *lovedness*, where our hearts are spiritually and emotionally healthy, that we produce laughter, which makes us physically healthier. In a world that wants to turn us all into rats and force us to run around until we're exhausted, God has a better way, a better plan. He offers us His love and the laughter it produces. This offer will empower us to live better and maybe, just maybe, live longer.

"Wondrous is the strength of cheerfulness and its power of endurance. The cheerful man will do more in the same time, will do it better, will persevere in it longer, than the sad or sullen."[10]

Let's kick sad and sullen into touch. Let's determine to love, be loved and laugh as much as we can on the way.

### And finally,

An Irish priest wanted to raise money for his church. On being told there was a fortune in horse racing, decided to purchase a horse to enter into the races. However, at the local auction, the going price for a horse was so high, he ended up having to settle for a donkey. He figured that since he had it, he might as well enter it into the races. To his surprise, the donkey came in third. The next day the local paper carried the headline:

**Priest's Ass Shows**

The priest was so pleased with the donkey that he entered it in another race and this time it won! The local paper read:

**Priest's Ass Out Front**

The Bishop was so upset with this kind of publicity that he

---

10. Thomas Carlyle.

ordered the priest not to enter the donkey in another race. The next day the local paper headline read:

**Bishop Scratches Priest's Ass**

This was too much for the Bishop, so he ordered the priest to get rid of the donkey. The priest decided to give it to a nun in a nearby convent. The local paper, hearing the news, posted the following headline the next day:

**Nun Has Best Ass in Town**

The Bishop fainted. He informed the nun that she would have to get rid of the donkey, so she sold it to a farmer for ten pounds. The paper headline read:

**Nun Sells Ass for £10.00**

This was too much for the Bishop, so he ordered the nun to buy back the donkey and lead it to the meadows where it could run wild. The next day the headlines read:

**Nun Announces Her Ass is Wild and Free**

The Bishop was buried a week later!

Laugh more and live well. You are loved!

# Chapter 11
## You'll Never Walk Alone

"God soon turns from his wrath,
but he never turns from his love."[1]

In 1956, Claramae Turner recorded a song from the movie, *Carousel*. Written by Oscar Hammerstein II and Richard Rodgers, it was given a new lease of life by Gerry and the Pacemakers in the 1960s and adopted by Liverpool football club as their official anthem. The title of the song adorns the entrance gates of the ground. Most Liverpool supporters probably wouldn't know who wrote it, but they do know how to sing it.

Being a childhood Liverpool supporter, I had the joy of visiting Anfield, their home ground, for a cup match. I managed to get a seat in the famous Kop, behind the goal. Although the match didn't start until 3.00pm, I was in my seat by 2.15pm taking it all in. As kick-off approached the music started and suddenly everyone around me stood to their feet and started to sing. One bloke behind me sang *badly* at the top of his lungs, breathing all over me as he did so. He had already consumed a number of cans of beer and by the time he finished singing, *I felt* drunk! I looked around at almost 45,000 people singing in unison, hands aloft,

---

1. Charles Haddon Spurgeon.

holding scarves and singing as if their lives depended on it. Some were crying, others had large veins sticking out of reddened necks as they gave the *holy* moment everything they had. We could have been in church, the worship was so passionate and intense. The song started slowly and gently, building to a great crescendo:

*Walk on, walk on with hope in your heart*

*And you'll nev – er walk a – lone,*

*You'll nev – er walk a – lone.*

Let me just wipe the tears from my eyes. Great song, powerful message, but the thing that has always confused me about this song is that it doesn't mention why we'll never walk alone. It tells me I won't, but I want to know why! This song evokes so much passion because its message is powerful. Every human on this planet wants, deep down inside, to believe they aren't alone; that someone, somewhere is with them, looking after them or watching out for them. As a result, people carry charms, go to church, talk to mediums, read horoscopes, believe in aliens and embrace social media in all its forms for connection. We like our space, we want our freedom, but we don't want to be *alone*.

The God who is love makes a promise to each one of us, as we reach out to Him by faith and dare to believe what He has said:

*"Never will I leave you; Never will I forsake you."* (Hebrews 13:5) In politics the rule is "Never say never" because "never" is a huge word that requires incredible power and commitment to work through. Yet, in the space of one sentence, God says "never" twice. Both times they are in the context of His commitment, love and loyalty to us. When we truly understand what that means, it has the power to revolutionise our lives. Some will read it the wrong way and attempt to abuse such favour, but others will grasp the potent reality of an inexhaustible statement of faithfulness, made

by a God who has the power to make it happen. Think about it for just a moment: the God described by John as love makes a promise to you that He will never leave or abandon you – that no matter where you go and whatever happens, He'll be there. God's awesome love is made manifest in a demonstration of incalculable faithfulness. He has promised to be with us, and He will. He has promised never to leave us, and He won't.

I was teaching a group of children a wonderful song about the faithfulness of God when the inevitable happened. A little seven year old girl put her hand up and asked, "What does faithfulness mean?" I had just left Bible College after three years of theological training with a diploma in biblical studies with Greek texts and a distinction in my hand. I was confident I had the answer somewhere – I just couldn't find where. I was about to be humiliated by a group of children when suddenly a flash of inspiration flooded into my mind.

I answered with a calmness that masked my panic: "Faithfulness means God will never let you down." The kids seemed happy with that and so was I. Many have been let down and abandoned by the god they made in their own image, by the god of their imagination and selfish desire. But no-one, not even you, has ever been let down by the God of love who promised to be faithful. If He's not there it's because *we* have stopped looking. If He's not in our life it's because we stopped inviting Him to tea. If He doesn't answer our prayers it's because *we* stopped praying or only expect the answer we want. He hasn't left the building… *we* have!

Tony Campolo grew up in a rough neighbourhood and it was dangerous for him to walk to school by himself. His mother used to pay an older girl called Harriet five cents a day to ensure her young son got to and from school safely. As he got older he became aware of the money being paid out on his behalf, so he suggested to his mother that she pay him the five cents instead and he be left to get to school on his own. After a lot of begging, Tony's mother agreed and he launched into a new era of independence. Years later, he was at a family get together and reminded his sisters of how strong and independent he had been. They laughed at him. "Did you think that you went to school alone and came home alone? Every day when you left the house Mom followed you and when you came out of school at the end of the day, she was there. She always made sure you didn't notice her, but she watched over you coming and going, just to make sure you were safe and nobody hurt you. She would follow you home then sneak in the back door. When she opened the front door and let you in, you were always left with the impression that you had been on your own, when in reality she had been watching over you all the time."[2]

Read the words again, *"Never will I leave you, never will I forsake you."*

They are not words of license, they are words of life. If these words can become a revelation to us, our lives will change forever.

## No P.S

A man walked into a photography studio with a framed picture of his girlfriend. He wanted the picture duplicated. This involved removing it from the frame. As he did so, the studio owner noticed the inscription on the back of the photograph:

"My dearest Tom, I love you with all my heart. I love you more and more each day. I will love you forever and ever. I am yours for all eternity, Diane."

However, it contained a P.S: "If we ever break up, I want this picture back."[3]

2. Campolo, op.cit., *Story*, pp.9-10.
3. John & Stibbe, op.cit., *Delights*, p.67.

I was married in 1988 and although I have had an incredibly wonderful life with my wife Dawn, when we analyse the promises couples make on the day of their wedding, they are not only beautiful but also a little scary. We say, "... for better, for worse, for richer for poorer, in sickness and in health, to love and to cherish until death us do part..." In a wedding ceremony no P.S is offered and there's no get-out clause. The idea is that the promises being made are for life. Some people, due to many different reasons, have found these promises impossible to keep. The trend today is to have a pre-marriage or pre-nuptial agreement in place, "just in case" something goes wrong. The pre-nup will ensure we can all be happy. I understand this mind-set, but it defeats the purpose of the vows being made. Love is a risk and life will not get lived without some trying times. If love is to succeed, there can be no PS in our thinking.

God has not written a secret P.S. What He has to say to us and what He has promised, He has put on the page for all to see. There is no small print, hidden agenda or get-out clause – it's all there and He's all in. If the "marriage" falls apart it won't be because He's walked out and found someone He loves more than us. It won't be because He's had enough of us. Rather, it will be because we decided we needed a change and He was top of the list. Those who have drifted away from God will rarely see it like that, but how else is there to see it? He's here... where are you? This does not mean God will put up with any old behaviour, as we've already said. As a loving *husband* He addresses Himself to our sin and failure, but not by abandoning us! He promises never to walk out the door. He promises never to leave us high and dry. He promises He will never renege on His love and duty to us.

Read these words and see if you can spot a P.S:

*"If we died with Him, we will also live with Him;*
*If we endure, we will also reign with Him.*
*If we disown Him, He will also disown us;*
*If we are faithless, He will remain faithful, for He cannot disown*
*Himself."*
(2 Timothy 2:11-13)

"Well John, line three looks like a PS to me." On first reading it does. If you took this line on its own that is exactly what it is, but then we read line four. There is no contradiction as both are compatible. If we choose to walk away from God, deny all knowledge of Him and reject His love and truth, then in justice, God will have no alternative but to affirm and confirm us in our chosen course by *rejecting* us. However, this rejection is only reflective of the choice *we* have already made, not of the heart of God in reaching out to us, hence the declaration of faithfulness which follows. Even if we disown Him and remain faithless, God will remain faithful, ever keeping His arms open for the day we choose to return. If we want to leave He will let us go, but when we turn and call to Him, He will always hear us and be there, because He never left in the first place.

The story is told of a Spanish father and son who became estranged. The son left home and the father later set out to find him. He searched for months with no success. Finally, in desperation, the father turned to the newspaper for help. His ad simply read, "Dear Paco, meet me in front of this newspaper office at noon on Saturday. All is forgiven. I love you. Your father."

On Saturday, 800 young men named Paco showed up looking for forgiveness and love from their estranged fathers.[4]

---

4. John & Stibbe, op.cit., *Fun*, p.68.

Your Father isn't going anywhere without you, so why should you go anywhere without Him?

## Did you think I would leave you dying?

One of my favourite songs growing up as a child was *Two Little Boys* and everyone in our house loved it. In fact, as a child, I knew every word off by heart. The song begins with two friends Jack and Joe, playing as children. As they pretend to be soldiers, Jack has a mishap and breaks the head off his wooden horse, but his friend Joe comes to the rescue (this is your cue to sing along):

> *Did you think I would leave you crying,*
> *when there's room on my horse for two.*
> *Climb up here Jack and don't be crying,*
> *I can go just as fast with two.*
> *When we grow up we'll both be soldiers,*
> *and our horses will not be toys,*
> *And I wonder if we'll remember,*
> *when we were two little boys.*

The two boys grow up and become soldiers, eventually fighting together. During the battle Joe is wounded and cries out for help. At this Jack gallops "out of the ranks so blue" to save his friend. As he reaches him, under heavy gunfire he sings these words:

> *Did you think I would leave you dying,*
> *when there's room on my horse for two.*
> *Climb up here Joe, we'll soon be flying,*
> *I can go just as fast with two.*

*Did you say Joe "I'm all a-tremble",*
*perhaps it's the battle's noise,*
*But I think it's that I remember,*
*when we were two little boys.*[5]


This simple little song was a hit in the UK popular music charts for seven weeks over Christmas 1969. But why? Perhaps it could have been the message it portrayed – one of love, loyalty and sacrifice – that deep down touched the hearts of those who heard it. That which they had as boys, they carried as men. As friends, in good times and bad, they were willing to risk all in love for each other. We all wish we had friends like this. Money can't buy them and only love can make them.

The truth is, we do have a friend like this, one who in times of adversity has promised to stick closer to us than a brother. Not only has God promised never to leave us but, incredibly, He actually wants to be with us. He doesn't stand passively in the background available only when we need Him. He engages with us longing to initiate love and friendship, showing and giving Himself to us.

Had I been Hosea's pastor, his remarkable story and profound prophetic words would never have been heard. "Well pastor, the reason I've come to see you is that God spoke to me last night. He told me to get married. His exact words were, 'Go, take to yourself an adulterous wife and children of unfaithfulness…'[6] I was wondering, are you free to do the wedding?"

Not only does Hosea marry Gomer, but a little later she leaves him for another man. God speaks to him again and tells him to go and fetch her back.

---

5. Morse - Madden arr. Braden) H. Darewski Music / EMI / Redwood Music (P) 1969 Cond. Alan Braden - Produced by Mickey Clarke.
6. Hosea 1:2.

*"Love her as the Lord loves the Israelites..."*[7]

Even a casual glance at the fourteen chapters of the book of Hosea reveal the heart of God. He's disappointed with the unfaithfulness of His people. He's grieved at the extent of their adultery, their lack of concern and love towards Him. He wants to punish them and threatens to do so, but even in the midst of His harshest words, He reaches out to them, willing to forgive them and longing to love them. Hosea's final words to the nation capture this powerfully.

*"Return, O Israel, to the Lord your God.*

*Your sins have been your downfall.*

*Take words with you and return to the Lord.*

*Say to Him: 'Forgive all our sins and receive us graciously, that we may offer the fruit of our lips...'"*

(Hosea 14:1-2)

In response to this, Hosea joyfully proclaims God's intentions:

*"I will heal their waywardness and love them freely, for my anger has turned away from them."* (Hosea 14:4)

The nation deserved nothing but desertion and punishment. They had treated their *Father* and *Husband* with complete contempt. Yet, as they lay wounded and broken, abused by the lovers who had so cruelly let them down, He offers Himself again to them, in the hope that they will once again love Him and allow Him to love them.

Another prophet speaking to God's people put it this way:

*"'Come now, let us reason together,' says the Lord. 'Though your sins are like scarlet, they shall be as white as snow; though they are red as crimson, they shall be like wool.'"* (Isaiah 1:18)

---

7. Hosea 3:1.

He will never leave us and never forsake us and He has promised that we will never walk alone. Even when we fail in sin, He is there for us. We will experience the full weight of His love as we reach out to Him, repent and obey.

There will always be room on God's horse for you. The question is, do you want to get on it?

## Hell or high water

Herman was the youngest son of the Rosenblatt family and in 1939, when he was only twelve years old, he and his family were forced into a Polish ghetto by the Germans. By 1944, although he had managed to survive, his father, mother and numerous other members of his family had not. He was a prisoner in a concentration camp outside Berlin called Schlieben, where under horrific circumstances, life was a daily struggle. Fed only on one slice of bread and water, hunger was the order of the day, with only sleep supplying relief. One day as he walked near the perimeter fence, a little girl caught his eye as she stood and stared at the camp. He asked her if she had anything to eat and without saying a word, she took out an apple and threw it at him. Herman caught the apple and started to run away, but as he did so he heard the little girl shout, "See you tomorrow."

The nameless girl was true to her word. She returned every single day Herman was at the camp, bringing food for her Jewish friend. Then Herman was relocated to another camp where he was prepared for liquidation. On the day he was due to be executed, his camp was liberated by the Allies and in 1957, while living in America, he met a beautiful Polish girl called Roma on a blind date. In an unbelievable moment, Herman was reunited with the little *angel* who, in the darkest moments of his life, kept her promise of bringing him food every day, risking her life to save his. Her love for him defied the fences and denied the holocaust one more victim. They married and lived a long, loved-filled life together.[8]

The God of love turns up every day of our lives, hoping we will grant Him permission to lavish His love upon us. Many times, because of our pain or the challenges we face, we wander around without ever noticing He is there and miss out on the blessings He wants to bestow on us. We live behind the fence, convinced we are alone, when all the time He is with us!

God speaks to His people with words of immense comfort and commitment:

*"When you pass through the waters,*
*I will be with you;*
*And when you pass through the rivers,*
*they will not sweep over you.*
*When you walk through the fire,*
*you will not be burned;*
*The flames will not set you ablaze."*
(Isaiah 43:2)

The promise is not just that God will help us when the waters rise, but that He will actually get in the water with us, stand with us and empower us to overcome. He's not standing at the side, reaching out His hand, offering to pull us out, He's in the torrent with us, with the strength to lift us out or help us through.

When the three Hebrew boys were thrown into the furnace for refusing to bow to the golden image of King Nebuchadnezzar,

---

8. Thomas, R., *It's a Miracle*, UK, 2002, pp.187-192.

it was expected their demise would be swift. The fire was so hot that the soldiers who threw the young men into the furnace died. However, Shadrach, Meshach and Abednego did not die. They went into the fire, but not alone. An eyewitness commented,

*"Look! I see four men walking around in the fire, unbound and unharmed, and the fourth looks like a son of the gods."*

(Daniel 3:25)

I wonder who that could be?

Too often we get the impression that God steps into our lives and pulls us out of a situation or rescues us from an attack. God does not step into our lives, because in truth, He never left. He didn't only speak to the boys in the flames, He was in the flames with them.

David put it this way:

*"Even though I walk through the darkest valley,*
*I will fear no evil, **for You are with me**;*
*Your rod and your staff they comfort me."*
(Psalm 23:4)

What hope, what a promise… what love!

When we grasp this truth, it should fill us with awe, worship and love for our great God and King. Not only does He initiate His actions towards us, inspired by love. Not only does He give us all we need for life and godliness, but He promises to stay with us whatever happens, wherever we go and however tough it gets. When He stepped into our lives and vowed His love to us, there was no intention in His mind to ever turn away from or abandon us. When He makes a promise it's for keeps and when He turns up, it's because He intends to stay.

Thousands will sing the anthem *You'll Never Walk Alone* in the context of a game and in worship of their heroes. Perhaps it's time that we stood up and began to sing with everything that is in us about the God who is love – of the God who will never leave us. We truly will never walk alone.

A number of years ago, Dawn and I were invited out for supper to the home of one of the ladies who attended our church. Whilst there, I noticed a beautiful painting hanging on the wall. Though small, its simplicity and beauty drew my eye and I enquired as to where our host had purchased it. I discovered she was in fact the creator of the unsigned piece and I immediately asked if she could paint one for me.

A few months later, she and her husband came to our home for a meal, and she came bearing a gift of the painting I had so admired in her home. But here's the thing: there are two ways of looking at the painting. Some glance at it from a distance, while others venture a little closer and discover the details, which are not easily recognizable at first, distant glance. For example, on the beach the artist has intricately painted a wonderful little starfish, as a personal touch just for me. This can't even be seen from a few feet away. To see it and appreciate its beauty, one has to get a lot closer.

In a sense, that is what this simple book has attempted to do on the immense subject of the love of God. A thousand chapters – or books for that matter – could not even begin to tax the reservoir of greatness that is His love. However, I have attempted, in a few short chapters, to reposition you a little closer to the *painting* in the hope that you will see things you've never seen before.

The love of God is magnificent from wherever you see it, but when we venture nearer, when we see it up close and personal, we understand and experience things, which cannot be appreciated from a distance.

Having read this book and got to the final page, my prayer is that you have moved a little closer, discovered a little more of His great love and are now living in a deeper sense of your *lovedness*. If that has happened, then my ramblings have succeeded and my ambition in making a difference to even one person has been realised! I pray like the great Apostle of old that you will discover the "extravagant dimensions" of His love, for this alone has the power to change your heart and the world you inhabit.

You are loved!